1-79

Introduction
to Labor

INTRODUCTION TO LABOR

JAMES W. ROBINSON

Virginia Polytechnic Institute
and State University

JAMES T. TURNER

Packaging Corporation of America

ROGER W. WALKER

Hamline University

Prentice-Hall, Inc., Englewood Cliffs, New Jersey

Library of Congress Cataloging in Publication Data

Robinson, James William, (date)
    Introduction to labor.

    Includes bibliographies and index.
    1. Industrial relations-United States.   2. Labor
economics.   I. Turner, James T., (date) joint author.
II. Walker, Roger W., joint author.   III. Title.
HD8072.R742   331   75-19424
ISBN0-13-485490-X

Printed in the United States of America

10   9   8   7   6   5   4   3

Prentice-Hall International, Inc., London
Prentice-Hall of Australia, Pty. Ltd., Sydney
Prentice-Hall of Canada, Ltd., Toronto
Prentice-Hall of India Private Limited, New Delhi
Prentice-Hall of Japan, Inc., Tokyo
Prentice-Hall of Southeast Asia (Pte.) Ltd., Singapore

To Our Wives

Contents

3

Poverty and Income Security   19

4

Government Regulation of the Labor Market   35

5

American Unions: Their Historical Development   47

6

The Unions Today   63

Preface

One of the most important factors in the determination of a nation's economic health and well-being is its labor force. Therefore, it is important for students, policy makers, and the general public to understand the dimensions of our labor force, the laws and regulations which govern its employment, the programs for its improvement and protection, the organizations to which it belongs, and the ways in which its employment is administered. This book is intended to assist in that understanding in terms and in language that are meaningful to persons who do not possess extensive educational backgrounds in economics, mathematics, and industrial management.

The first three chapters introduce the reader to labor as a concept and as an economic resource that is bought (by employers) and sold (by workers in exchange for wages) through the mechanism of a marketplace. Chapter Four elaborates some of the ways in which the government regulates that marketplace. Chapters Five through Eleven trace, within an historical-institutional context, the evolution of labor-management relations from our early history to the present time. Finally, Chapter Twelve offers the reader insights into the various ways in which employers attempt to use their labor forces most efficiently.

At the end of each chapter, the reader is provided with a reminder of the important new terms introduced in that chapter, as well as with notes and suggested additional readings to direct further research into a particular topic.

The authors are indebted to their colleagues at Hamline University, Virginia Polytechnic Institute and State University, and the Packaging Corporation of America who have offered helpful suggestions and support during the preparation of this book. The authors appreciate the comments of Professors John P. DeLuca of Middlesex Community College, Gary W. Falkenberg of Oakland Community College, and Thomas G. Gutteridge of the State University of New York at Buffalo who reviewed the manuscript. The editorial staff of Prentice-Hall, particularly Mr. Paul McKenney, offered invaluable assistance. Ken Demarko, Robert L. Walker, and Eileen Lile provided valuable assistance in the preparation of the final manuscript and in typing.

Most of all, the authors are indebted to their parents who provided the impetus and resources for their education without which this book would not have been produced; and to our wives—Sandy Robinson, Judy Turner, and Bobbi Walker—whose understanding, encouragement, and most of all patience, enabled this book to be completed. The authors are, of course, responsible for any errors in the work.

January 1975

James W. Robinson
Salem, Virginia
James T. Turner
Rittman, Ohio
Roger W. Walker
St. Paul, Minnesota

Introduction
to Labor

1

Introduction

THE STUDY OF LABOR

The typical college student who is majoring in business administration, economics, or liberal arts will encounter a course related in some way to labor during his or her period of study. It may be entitled "labor relations," "labor economics," "personnel administration," or a variety of other names. The course is likely to include (among other topics) a study of employment and unemployment; unions in our economic system; various laws that affect workers and their employers; and aspects of industrial management that concern the hiring, promotion, and evaluation of employees. What many students may not realize is that such courses are comparatively recent additions to the curricula of most colleges, having been introduced during the past 50 years.

The study of employment trends and patterns and the reasons for and potential solutions to unemployment received an impetus from the Great Depression that began in 1929 when it became obvious that analysis of our major source of production—human labor—might alleviate some of the causes of economic recession.[1] The "New Deal" legislation which followed that depression created various governmental programs to deal with the human problems of employment, such as old age, disability, and unemployment.[2] Creation of these programs brought attention to the study of alternative solutions to these human problems. Although the pioneer efforts of persons like John R. Commons in the study of unions and labor-management relations began shortly after the beginning of the twentieth century, recognition of the importance of such studies awaited the passage of important labor legislation in 1935 and the rapid growth in union strength during and immediately after World War II.[3] The advent of "scientific management" created increased needs to study employees as important components of the production process in an effort to discover better means of increasing output.[4]

Each of these factors has been important in the expansion of course offerings in the field of labor. However, there are other, and more direct, reasons why students of business administration, economics, and other majors complete courses dealing with the subject matter of labor. Students learn about the opportunities in various industries and occupations as they begin to consider employment. Upon graduation, students enter the labor force and begin making contributions to the social security program and considering alternative approaches to the problems of potential disability, ill health, and unemployment. Most students will become managers and face some aspects of effective personnel administration. And the chances are approximately one in four that they will encounter a union that represents the employees of their firm. As citizens and voters, they will need to understand the statistics and stories in the media that report on unemployment, poverty, and education and the policies designed to cope with the issues.

THE MEANING OF LABOR

The term *labor* implies different ideas to various people. To the television reporter preparing a news story on a strike, *labor* connotes the union representing the striking employees and the labor organizations with which it is affiliated. To the employer seeking to improve his or her competitive position in the market, *labor* refers to a cost or a productive resource used in the manufacture of a product. To the politician or philosopher, *labor* is a description of the great mass of persons who work for wages as opposed to a wealthy few who derive their incomes from the ownership of property.

The employer in our example is thinking of *labor* as a factor of production like land or capital. As such, labor is treated as a commodity for which there is a demand and of which there is a supply. This supply and demand are equated by the price of labor—wages—in what is called the *labor market*. The initial chapters of the book concern the way in which the labor market functions, some of its imperfections, and some of the ways in which the government affects its functioning.

The politician and philosopher in our example were thinking of *labor* in terms synonymous with the "working class." This terminology is largely a political one in the United States. During the twentieth century, U.S. workers have sought not to eliminate any class structure but rather to share in the earnings of capital.[5] However, there has been increased recognition in this decade that there is a group of undereducated and unskilled persons who exist largely outside the mainstream of our labor force. The problems of this group and some of the proposals for solving them are discussed in Chapter 3. Some of the historical antecedents of the U.S. view of a "working class" are discussed in Chapter 5.

The television reporter in our example was equating *labor* with unions, or with *organized labor*. The role of organized labor in our society and economy is considered later in the book. We consider the historical evolution of organized labor, its present status, and the ways in which it relates to the employer-employee relationship.

INDUSTRIAL RELATIONS AND PERSONNEL MANAGEMENT

The term *industrial relations* is employed to describe the ways in which employers and the unions that represent their employees relate to one another. It includes, among others, the study of the ways in which unions function, the reasons why persons join unions, the negotiation of collective bargaining agreements, the administration of the agreements, methods of resolving disputes between the parties, and the legal environment of labor-management relations.

The term *personnel management* describes the study of ways in which employees are utilized most effectively. It includes the selection and recruitment of employees, their training, their motivation, criteria for establishing their wages and salaries, and the methods of evaluating their performance for purposes of retention and promotion. This study borrows from engineering the techniques of time and motion study; from psychology, the analyses of large and small group behavior; and from economics, the criteria for wage and salary structures.

Chapters 7 through 11 of this book are concerned with industrial relations, and Chapter 12 with personnel management. However, the student should not believe that there is a clear distinction between the two fields of study. There are many common characteristics; and most practitioners are familiar with the significant aspects of each.

The authors of this book believe that the study of labor in its many dimensions and definitions is one of the most interesting available to the student and that a career in labor relations or personnel management offers many rewards. Their effort in this book is to provide the student with an introduction to the major topics in the study of labor, each of which is often the subject of an entire course at many colleges and universities. Footnotes throughout the book are intended to suggest additional reading that the interested student may wish to pursue. At the end of each chapter are included important terms and their definitions which have been introduced in the respective chapters.

NOTES

[1] Foster Rhea Dulles, *Labor in America* (New York: Thomas Y. Crowell, 1949), Chapter XIV contains an interesting account of the depression and its effects on organized labor. A more lengthy account is contained in Irving Bernstein, *The Lean Years: A History of the American Worker 1920-1933* (Baltimore: Penguin Books, 1966).

[2] Milton Derber and Edwin Young (eds.), *Labor and the New Deal* (Madison: University of Wisconsin Press, 1961) offers a variety of facts and opinions on the "New Deal" programs affecting labor.

[3] Mark Perlman, *Labor Union Theories in America* (Evanston: Row, Peterson, 1958) develops the various theories of union growth and traces the development of the study of organized labor.

[4] Frederick W. Taylor's *Principles of Scentific Management* (New York: Harper, 1911) contains the most comprehensive accounts of this movement by its originator. An interesting critique of this movement and what has followed is provided in Daniel Bell, *Work and Its Discontents* (New York: League for Industrial Democracy, 1970).

[5] Jack Barbash (ed.), *Unions and Union Leadership* (New York: Harper, 1959) offers a selection of readings that provides considerable insight into the "style" of organized labor in the United States.

2

The Market
for Labor

SUPPLY OF AND DEMAND FOR LABOR

Role of the Labor Market

Government regulatory agencies establish the prices of some of the products that consumers purchase, such as the electric power they consume or the airline ticket they purchase. However, the prices of most of the goods and services that consumers purchase are determined, in varying degrees, by the demand for the good or the amount that consumers wish to purchase and by the supply or the amount that producers have available to sell. When the "energy crisis" arrived in 1973 the prices of subcompact automobiles increased because the number of persons seeking to purchase such automobiles exceeded the available supply. Similarly, the prices of full-sized automobiles decreased because the number of persons seeking to purchase them was less than the available supply. The prices of various types of automobiles were fluctuating in the automobile market in which buyers and sellers were brought together.

Labor is perhaps the most important commodity in any economy. It is purchased and sold like any other commodity with the only difference being a technical one, i.e., the effort or capacity of the commodity is purchased rather than the commodity itself. Employers are the purchasers of labor. Individual workers and the unions that represent them are the sellers of labor. They are brought together through the *labor market*. The prices of various types of labor

5

fluctuate in a manner similar to that of the automobiles mentioned above. When methods of production become more complex and require greater skills for operation employers demand more skilled workers. The price of skilled labor, or the wage rate for skilled labor, increases. The wage rate for unskilled labor decreases. Unless the unskilled workers acquire skills, the number of jobs or the amount of *employment* available for unskilled workers will be less than the number of unskilled workers seeking employment. The difference is called *unemployment*. The number of persons who are employed plus the number of persons who are unemployed equals the *labor force*.

Detailed statistics on the characteristics of the labor force and on unemployment are compiled by the Employment Services of the various states, the U.S. Department of Labor through its Bureau of Labor Statistics, and the U.S. Department of Commerce through its Census Bureau. These statistics form the basis for the study of historical changes and for projections of future changes. Study of these statistics and projected changes provides necessary information on training and educational needs and on needed improvements in the functioning of the labor market. Much of the remainder of this chapter is a description of these statistics and projections.[1]

SELECTED EMPLOYMENT STRUCTURES

The U.S. labor force consisted of some 93 million persons, or 62 percent of the total population, aged 16 years and older in 1974.[2] A little more than 50 million persons in this labor force were males, and 80.6 million were white. White-collar workers, particularly clerical workers, were the largest component of the labor force; farm workers, particularly farm laborers, were the smallest component. The service industries employed the largest number of persons and the mining industry, the smallest number.

Significant changes in the size and character of the labor force are anticipated in the next decade. These changes will involve the sex, age, and color distribution of workers; the industries in which they are employed; the occupations they have; and the area of the nation in which they live and work. Persons who study the labor force refer to these characteristics of it as the sex, age, color, industrial, occupational, and geographic *structures of the labor force.*

Age, Sex, and Racial Composition

The U.S. labor force is expected to grow at an annual rate of 1.7 percent until it exceeds 100 million persons in 1980, and to increase at about 1.2 percent annually until 1985 when it should reach a total of 107 million persons.[3] The largest increase among age groups will be persons 25 to 34 years old (Figure 1). Women will continue to enter the labor force in increasing

FIGURE 1   *Age Composition of the Labor Force, 1960-1985*

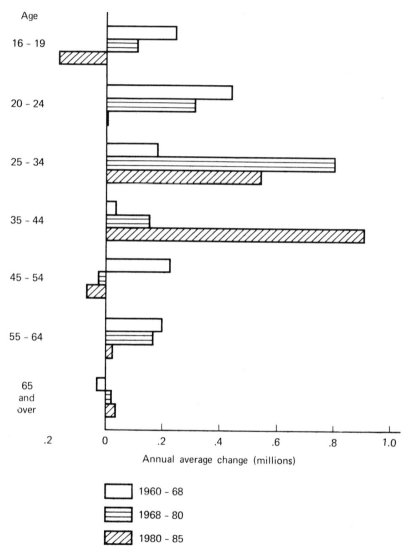

numbers and should constitute nearly 37 percent of it by 1985 (Figure 2). The percentage of blacks and other minority groups in the labor force will increase slightly because of greater population increases projected for those groups than for whites.[4]

Industrial Structure

The major change in the industrial structure of the labor force in this decade has been the shift to service-producing employment from goods-producing employment. The *service-producing* industry groups include services per se (e.g., household services, medical care, education, etc.); trade; government; transportation, communications, and public utilities; and finance, insur-

FIGURE 2   *Change in Total Labor Force, by Age and Sex, 1950 to 1980*

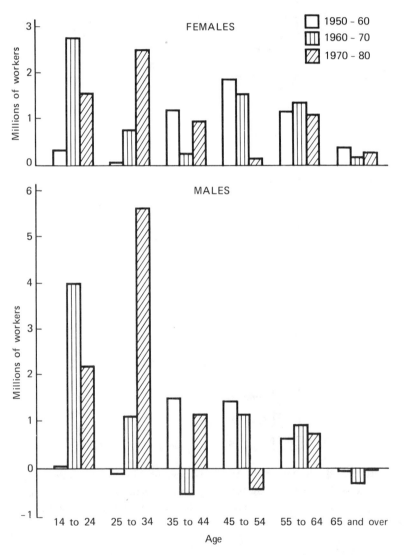

Source: Sophia Cooper and Denis F. Johnston, "Labor Force Projections for 1970-80," *Monthly Labor Review* (February 1965).

FIGURE 3   *Employment Trends and Projections to 1980*

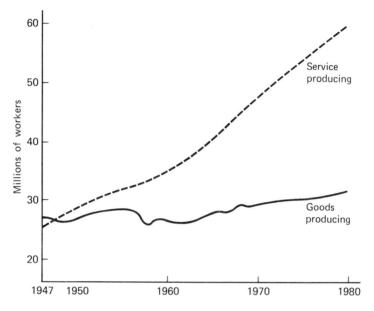

Source: *Monthly Labor Review* (April 1970)

ance, and real estate. Only three of every 10 workers were employed in services in 1900, but nearly seven of every 10 workers will be employed in them by 1980 (Figure 3).[5] *Government* employment, primarily state and local government employment, increased more than that in any other industrial sector during the 1960s. It will continue to increase but at a diminished rate. Public demands for governmental services continue to increase as public concerns about the environment, energy, health, old-age, and other matters increase.

Employment in business, personal, health, and educational *services* will increase from 18.7 percent of total employment to 21 percent by 1980.[6] Employment may increase by as much as 100 percent in business services because of expanded advertising, consumer credit, and all types of records. As consumer incomes increase, consumers' demands for recreational, health, and other services will increase also.

Employment increases in the trade and the finance, insurance, and real estate sectors should parallel those in total employment with no significant increases in their shares of total employment. Increased use of electronic data processing, automated inventory control systems, and other labor-saving techniques is responsible for the lack of significant growth in these sectors.

The percentage of persons employed in *transportation, communications,* and *public utilities* will decrease in 1980.[7] Increased employment in trucking and air transportation should equal decreases in railroad employment. Employment by public utilities has limited growth because of increased output per man-hour which enables the same number of employees to produce increased outputs.

There will be a moderate increase in employment for the *goods-producing* industry groups by 1980, reflecting decreased employment in some sectors and increased employment in others. Increased productivity will combine with an only slight increase in demand to decrease employment in *agriculture* from 5.1 percent to only 3.2 percent of total employment in 1980.[8] Similar factors should also produce decreased employment in *mining* although a continued petroleum shortage and resulting shift to coal could change this projection. Increased demand for housing should increase *construction* employment despite increased productivity resulting from techniques such as prefabrication.

Manufacturing should remain the largest source of employment in the economy.[9] However, employment will not increase as rapidly as in the past because of increased use of labor-saving equipment and technological innovations in many manufacturing industries.

Occupational Structure

The projected changes in the occupational structure of employment (Figure 4) reflect the changes in industrial employment as well as changes in the employment requirements within a given industry. Employment may increase significantly in a given firm because of an increase in the demand for its product. However, the increased production may be accomplished by sophisticated new equipment. The result will be an increase in employment of engineers and technicians rather than in employment of the firm's traditional production-line work force.

Labor economists and statisticians distinguish between two general categories of occupations—white-collar workers and blue-collar workers. The former category includes professional, technical, clerical, and sales workers; managers; and proprietors. The latter category includes craftsmen, foremen, operatives,[10] and nonfarm laborers. Service workers and farm workers comprise two additional categories, which account for smaller amounts of employment and include both white-collar and blue-collar workers.

Professional, technical, and similar occupations have demonstrated the largest growth in employment during recent decades and will increase at a rate twice that of overall employment growth during the 1970s.[11] Employment in these occupations will increase from 13.6 percent of total employment in 1968 to 16.3 percent in 1980 if projections are accurate.

Clerical employment will also increase at a rate above that of total employment. Clerical employment should increase from 16.9 percent of total employment in 1968 to 18.2 percent in 1980. The expected growth of the finance, insurance, and real estate industries, which employ many clerical workers, is a primary factor in this anticipated employment increase.[12]

FIGURE 4   *Projected Employment in Major Occupational Groups*

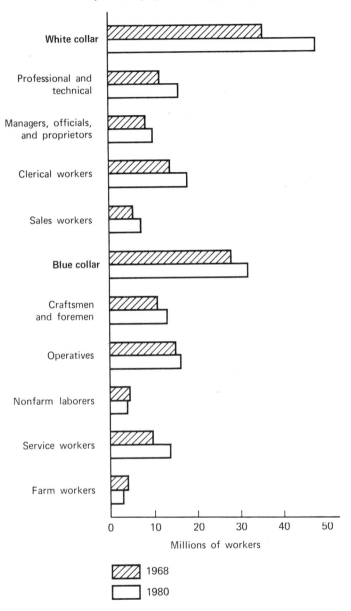

Source: *Monthly Labor Review* (April 1970)

Craftsmen, foremen, others in similar occupations, and *semiskilled workers* will experience employment increases at rates less than those of total employment. This result derives, in part, from the slow increases in manufacturing employment, the segment in which the largest percentage of operatives and semiskilled workers are employed.

Changed techniques of merchandising will slow the expansion of employment in *sales* occupations, leaving employment in those occupations at about 6 percent of total employment. *Nonfarm laborers* will decrease from 4.7 percent of total employment to 3.7 percent by 1980 because of continued substitution of machines for unskilled labor. The number of *farm laborers* will decrease by one-third as technological innovations continue to create labor-saving equipment for agriculture.

The rate of increase in employment of *services workers* will be approximately 50 percent more than that for total employment as population, incomes, and leisure time increase.[13] Health service employment will increase by the largest percentage, and private household service employment by the smallest.

Geographical Structure

Although the labor force is projected to increase in all regions and states during the 1970s, the rates of growth vary from 7.4 percent in Rhode Island to 36.3 percent in Arizona, and from 12.3 percent in the Northeast to 25.7 percent in the West (Table 1 and Figure 5).

TABLE 1

Labor Force Increases, 1960-70 and Projected Increases, 1970-1980, by Region

Region	1960-70 Increase	Projected Increase, 1970-80
	(percentages)	
Northeast	15.8	12.3
North Central	16.7	16.9
South	25.4	19.3
West	35.5	25.7
United States	22.0	18.1

Source: *Monthly Labor Review* (October 1966)

FIGURE 5   *Percentage Increases in Projected Labor Forces of the States, 1970-1980*

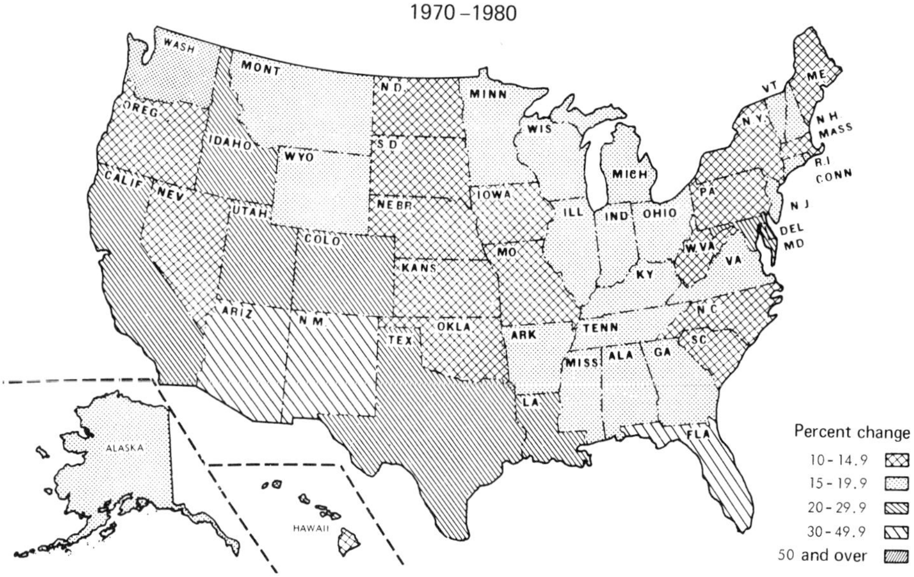

1970–1980

Source: *Monthly Labor Review* (October 1966)

UNEMPLOYMENT

Causes and Cures

The labor force includes two groups of persons, those who are employed and those who are *unemployed*. We have considered the various industries and occupations in which the employed persons work in the preceding section. The unemployed persons are those who are not working, but all persons who are not working are not unemployed. A woman who stays at home to care for her children while her husband is at work is not unemployed. A severely retarded person living in an institution is not unemployed. A former coal miner in a depressed area who cannot sell his home and who cannot afford the move to an area in which he might obtain a job is not unemployed. In fact, none of these individuals is in the labor force; and persons who are not in the labor force cannot be unemployed.

Economists and statisticians both in and out of our government accept generally the requirement that four criteria must be satisfied before an individual is considered to be unemployed. These criteria are that the individual be:[14]

1. Willing to work, i.e., that the individual is prepared to accept a job reasonably suited to his or her abilities;

2. Able to work, i.e., that the individual is mentally and physically qualified for employment and possesses the skill and/or education necessary for some type of employment;

3. Seeking to work, i.e., that the individual is making some attempt to find employment; but

4. Not working, i.e., that the individual is not employed despite his or her possession of ability and his or her willingness and effort to find work.

The housewife in our example is not in the labor force because she is not seeking work. The retarded individual living in an institution is not able to work. The former coal miner is not willing to work because he cannot accept employment in an area other than that in which he resides.

There are two additional types of employment status that exist apart from the two general categories of employed and unemployed persons. Persons who are employed in a job with skill or education requirements less than those which they possess are *underemployed* or considered to be a part of *disguised* unemployment. These individuals are employed because they have jobs, but they are not employed in jobs that utilize fully their abilities and training. Therefore, they constitute a resource that is not employed fully, or one which is underemployed. Persons whose hours of work are reduced involuntarily below normal constitute *concealed unemployment.* They may, for example, be employed for only 20 hours per week instead of their normal 40 hours. They are resources not fully employed but do not appear in the unemployment statistics because their 20 hours per week of unemployment is concealed.

Types of Unemployment

A variety of categories of unemployment have been defined. However, labor economists agree generally on a division of unemployment into four categories based on the causes of the unemployment and the characteristics of the unemployment.[15] *Cyclical* unemployment results when the demands of consumers for goods and services is not sufficient to require the employment of most of the persons who are willing, able, and seeking to work. In other words, it is unemployment that occurs when there are serious and general problems throughout the economy that result in what we refer to as a recession or depression. Cyclical unemployment is usually widespread throughout all industries and occupations and tends to continue for long periods of time when the direction of the business cycle is down. Cyclical unemployment was present when one person out of four in the labor force was unemployed during the depression that began in 1929.

By contrast, *structural* unemployment is not widespread and does not affect all industries and occupations and may occur at a time of general economic prosperity. An example of structural unemployment occurred in the post-World War II period when consumers shifted from coal to other energy sources and coal mining experienced greatly increased mechanization with the result that large numbers of coal miners in Appalachia were left without employment. This type of unemployment is persistent and usually of long duration because it involves a fundamental "imbalance" in the labor market, e.g., large numbers of persons who possess sets of skills no longer in demand exist at the same time that many job openings are available and unfilled for persons who possess a different set of skills.

Seasonal unemployment occurs regularly because of regular variations in consumer demand for certain products, the weather, and the fact that entries into and exits from the labor force by large numbers of persons tend to be concentrated at certain times of the year. Large numbers of students enter the labor force each June, and unemployment increases; large numbers of the same students leave the labor force each September, and unemployment decreases. Agricultural employment and unemployment relate to regular variations in weather. This type of unemployment is usually of short duration and poses no serious problems for an otherwise healthy economy. Most unemployment statistics are "seasonally adjusted" to allow for this factor. Otherwise, unemployment statistics might, for example, be too high in June and too low in September.

Frictional unemployment results from the ability of persons in a free economy to change jobs. Some persons will always be "between jobs" and, therefore, counted as unemployed because of this factor. This type of unemployment poses no serious problem in a healthy economy and is regarded generally as a price for the freedom to select one's employment.

Some unemployment or "normal unemployment" of 3 to 6 percent of the labor force is expected in even a healthy and dynamic economy because of the existence of frictional and seasonal unemployment and a limited amount of structural unemployment. However, concern increases when unemployment exceeds what is considered "normal" and large numbers of persons are without work for considerable periods of time. The federal government maintains current statistics on employment and unemployment in order to determine the amount and types of unemployment and any needed remedies. Monthly surveys by the U.S. Department of Labor and the Census Bureau are supplemented by reports from the state employment services on the number of persons who register for unemployment insurance benefits.

If the government determines that unemployment is primarily cyclical, it can take monetary and fiscal measures to stimulate the economy and create jobs. Taxes may be reduced to give consumers more money to spend on goods and services. Interest rates may be decreased to encourage spending instead of saving. Government spending for goods and services may be increased. Inherent in these measures is the assumption that increased spending creates a need for employment in order to produce the goods and services for which spending increases.

If the government determines that unemployment is primarily structural, specific measures must be designed to solve the problems of the groups of
workers involved. Programs of education and retraining that will provide the
unemployed persons with capabilities for available jobs may be instituted.
Programs to assist unemployed workers in relocation to geographic areas in
which jobs are available for them may be developed.[16] Cooperative programs
with industries and firms to provide on-the-job training are another alternative.

Within each of the various types of unemployment groups there exist
persons whose unemployment rate is higher than that of the overall labor force.
Members of minority groups, women, teenagers, older workers, and persons with
limited education experience more difficulty in finding employment than other
persons (Table 2).

TABLE 2

**Unemployment Rates for
Selected Population Groups, 1972**

Group	Rate of Unemployment
	(percentage)
All persons aged 16 or older	5.6
White males	4.9
White females	6.6
Nonwhite males	8.9
Nonwhite females	11.3
White teenagers	14.2
Nonwhite teenagers	33.5

Source: *Manpower Report of the President, 1973*

Various private and governmental efforts to ensure equal employment
and educational opportunities for all persons have produced some success. The
difference between the unemployment rates of white males and black males has
decreased considerably in the past decade, but the difference between those of
white and black females has change little.[17] The difference between the
unemployment rates of white and black teenagers has increased. The plight of
the person with limited education, regardless of his or her race or age, is perhaps
the most desperate. The situation is described well by Sumner Myers:[18]

> In an increasingly technological society, functional illiterates pay a
> heavy price for their handicap. Today, 50 percent of the young adults
> who are unemployed cannot read well enough to hold a job requiring
> reasonable skills, and there are fewer and fewer unskilled jobs . . .
> Current estimates indicate that unskilled laborers will be able to handle
> only 5 percent of all jobs . . . .

The high unemployment of these groups of persons represents a loss in potential productive resources of the economy, a social cost for the nation's taxpayers, and a source of shame for the world's wealthiest nation. In the next chapter, we shall consider some of the special problems of various groups in our population and some of the programs designed to solve these problems.

IMPORTANT NEW TERMS INTRODUCED

Labor force: The total of the number of persons who are employed and the number of persons who are not working but who are willing, able, and seeking to work.

Underemployment: The persons who are employed in jobs that require less ability than they possess.

Concealed unemployment: Persons whose hours of work are reduced involuntarily below normal.

SUGGESTED ADDITIONAL READINGS

Eli Ginzberg, *Manpower Agenda for America* (New York: McGraw-Hill, 1968).

Manpower Report of the President (Washington: U.S. Government Printing Office) for the current year.

NOTES

[1] Some useful insights on the ways people look for employment and the ways employers seek workers are contained in Glenn W. Miller, Harry H. Round, Frederick A. Zeller, and Terrence E. Wheaton, *Use of and Attitudes Toward the Ohio Bureau of Unemployment Compensation* (Columbus: Ohio State Research Foundation, 1963).

[2] *Monthly Labor Review* (April 1975), p. 92.

[3] Sophia C. Travis, "The U.S. Labor Force: Projections to 1985," *Monthly Labor Review* (February 1970), pp. 3-12.

[4] Ibid. Also see Sophia Cooper and Denis F. Johnston, "Labor Force Projections by Color, 1970-80," *Monthly Labor Review* (September 1966), pp. 965-972.

[5] "The United States Economy in 1980," *Monthly Labor Review* (April 1970), p. 15.

[6] Ibid., pp. 16-17.

[7] Ibid., p. 15.

[8] Ibid., p. 17.

[9] Ibid., p. 18.

[10] The term "operatives" refers to semiskilled workers, such as factory assemblers, equipment operators, drivers, etc.

[11] "The United States Economy in 1980," p. 21.

[12] Ibid., p. 22.

[13] Ibid., p. 24.

[14] See Robert L. Stein, "New Definitions for Employment and Unemployment," *Employment and Earnings and Monthly Report on the Labor Force* (February 1967), reprinted by the U.S. Department of Labor, Bureau of Labor Statistics.

[15] See U.S. Congress, Joint Economic Committee, *Unemployment: Technology, Measurement, and Analysis,* 87th Cong., 1st sess., 1961.

[16] For example, see John L. Fulmer and James W. Robinson, "Worker Mobility and Government Aid," *Business and Government Review* (September-October 1966), pp. 14-22.

[17] *Manpower Report of the President, 1973* (Washington: U.S. Government Printing Office, 1973), pp. 20-21.

[18] Sumner Myers, "For All Our Children—'The Right to Read,' " *Looking Ahead* (June 1970).

3

Poverty
and
Income Security

INTRODUCTION

Poverty has apparently been with mankind as long as there has been any type of social structure. Poverty is a relative occurence, i.e., presumably an income distribution exists in all societies within whose context people can be identified as "rich" or "poor." It is important to realize that poverty becomes a problem when society decides that it has become a problem and decides to devote its attention to poverty. It can be argued that what society decides to do about poverty is a political decision also. This process and the techniques used historically and currently are the subjects of this chapter.

Although poverty is certainly very old[1] its presence in a political sense was not recognized in this country until the early 1960s. The *Economic Report of the President* for 1964 contained the first "official" federal government recognition of poverty's existence. Much has been written about how "poor" one must be in order to be included in the poverty category. It is important to recognize that the reason $3,000 was employed by the President's Council of Economic Advisors in the early 1960s to define "poverty" for an urban family of four persons and gained such widespread use and acceptance was because it was used by persons with personal political credibility.

By way of general introduction, the concept of *effective regulation* must be developed briefly. "Regulation" is a rather benign and therefore acceptable form of government intervention for most Americans, frequently in the form of some permanent governmental agency established to solve a specific problem like public utility regulation. This attitude has been carried sometimes to the extreme of assuming that if government has created an agency to regulate an activity, that activity *is*, in fact, regulated. The principle is a simple one: if society chooses to regulate, the assumption is that the regulation is effective. The presence of that regulation becomes the major barrier to development of more effective regulation. This brief discussion of effective and ineffective regulation may be significant to our assessment of U.S. efforts to combat poverty. The persistent continuation of large numbers of persons in poverty is difficult to explain by arguing that there are insufficient numbers of antipoverty programs. The answer must be elsewhere.

OLD AND NEW FACES OF ECONOMIC INSECURITY

Despite the longevity of economic insecurity, its nature has changed in two respects as urban industrialization has become the dominant characteristic of western society. First, urban industrial poverty is a problem that must be met, but rural agricultural poverty "hides" or is forced to hide. Second, each type of poverty is caused by different factors. Rural poverty is caused by either occasional natural disasters or the forcing of farm families onto marginal land. This poverty is likely to be relatively short-lived and easily absorbed by society without any additional formal structure. By contrast, urban industrial poverty is caused by either temporary or permanent economic occurrences (e.g., unemployment versus physical disability) or by structural flaws in the economy, such as the long-term inability of given subcultural groups like blacks to participate effectively in normal economic activities. This type of poverty generally produces, among other things, special socioeconomic structures to accommodate it. As industrialization continues, society develops programs to meet the problems posed by new risks. Thus, a variety of attempts were made (culminating in workmen's compensation) to deal with the risk of industrial (on-the-job) injuries, accidents, and deaths; and unemployment insurance was developed during the depression of the 1930s.[2] The fact that the personal or family result of the occurrence of these risks is exactly the same—incomes are reduced and eventually a group of poor people is created in society—was neglected.

Another problem generated by this type of specific approach is that the solution does not provide any type of assistance for those persons whose income is low for some reason that has not been specified by the programs. Therefore, although it is at least theoretically possible that these programs might deal effectively with poverty created by industrialization, they cannot, by definition, deal with the other types of poverty. This inability explains the variety of attempts to deal with poverty as a much broader phenomenon, beginning with the Kennedy-Johnson administration.

TRADITIONAL INCOME MAINTENANCE STRUCTURES[3]

Traditional approaches to income maintenance in the U.S. have been highly specific and "keyed" to the presumed source or cause of income shortage or interruption. As a prelude to examination of these programs, it is appropriate to analyze briefly the different theories which are the bases for what is being done currently and has been done for some time, through traditional social welfare programs.[4] It is clear that no one of the concepts has dominated our income maintenance programs. Instead several concepts have been simultaneously significant in our history.

The first of these concepts is the simple notion that the way to eradicate poverty,[5] or at least to reduce it to an absolute minimum, is to make it as unattractive as possible. The logic of this notion is that the majority of persons who become poor had a real choice. The choice was presumed to be between being poor and nonpoor. Apparently, poverty appeared to be the more attractive alternative; so people decided to become poor. The obvious solution to the dilemma is to make poverty the less attractive alternative. This policy has been followed at various times in the U.S. For example, the use of institutions like county poor homes in some areas as late as the 1950s was motivated undoubtedly by considerations of economy and the desire to reduce the attractiveness of public support. A more contemporary example of the same logic was the practice by some state and county welfare agencies of making public the names of welfare recipients.

The second of these concepts is the apparently simple observation that the problem with poor people is that they possess and exercise the wrong set of values. This observation is complex and rather sophisticated. It argues alternatively that the poor do not want to work, or at least to work enough. Presumably if the poor had acquired the "proper" values, one of which is a respect for work, they would not be poor. This view argues that if the poor were to apply or follow the values of the nonpoor, they would become nonpoor.[6] It extends to matters other than simple work also. It is argued, for example, that the improper values of the poor are reflected in the way that they manage those funds which they do receive. Popular thinking has maintained that the poor spend their money on the "wrong" things. The wonderful aspect of this argument is its tendency to be both circular and self-affirming. It is argued that the poor spend their money on the wrong things because they would not be poor if they spent their money on the "right" things. If they are poor, it follows that they must have spent their money on the wrong things. This logic has moved many past and present public welfare programs to attempt to save the poor from themselves *by giving them as little cash as possible!* Public welfare recipients are provided food stamps, agency-paid medical care, etc. Although the reason for providing recipients with services instead of cash may be the direct saving in administrative expense, no small part of the logic is a concern for what the recipient might spend money for if he were given cash. Limitations on the items for which food stamps may be used are an example of this thinking.[7] What is really being argued is that the poor are incompetent to manage their own affairs. If they were not, after all, they would not be poor.

The third concept is frequently called the "worthy poor." Originally developed in many of Charles Dickens' novels, it maintains that some poor persons deserve public support because they are poor for a reason that is beyond their control. This concept identifies the old, the blind, the permanently and totally disabled, and young children as "worthy poor" in the U.S. By contrast, other poor persons are poor for the "wrong" reasons and should be viewed with at least some degree of suspicion. Having identified the worthy poor, this concept holds that these persons should be supported with public funds but supported at a level only slightly above that necessitated by physiological needs, i.e., subsistence.

The most recent notion to emerge is one that seeks to transform poor people into much more efficient economic units. It argues that the basic cause of poverty is the inability of poor people to function effectively as producers and consumers of income. The solution proposed is simple, i.e., the transformation of these inefficient persons into much more efficient ones. Many of the programs which comprised both the "War on Poverty" and its predecessor, the assault on depressed areas, were founded in this notion of economic transformation. For example, a major component of the "War on Poverty" consisted of programs whose purposes were to train, retrain, geographically relocate, and generally make more functional a large group of persons from the poverty groups. The major apparent shortcoming of this approach was the general tendency of the public to grossly underestimate the difficulty involved in these activities. In reality, the training or retraining process often involves taking individuals who are functionally illiterate and proceeding through the entire process of teaching them to read and to write, to do basic arithmetic and similar functions, and finally to acquire sufficient skill or knowledge to perform adequately on a job. Although it is often frustrating to fully disclose to the public the difficulties and shortcomings of any process for which public political support is being sought, such efforts are essential in the long run.

Having reviewed these concepts as general background, we now briefly consider the operation of the major traditional income maintenance programs of our society. A brief summary of each program will be provided, including a review of its goals, its eligibility requirements, its total benefit impact, and some assessment of its strengths and weaknesses. It is well to remember that the general working of U.S. income maintenance programs makes *any* expectation that any program will provide its beneficiaries with an adequate income unrealistic *unless* those persons provided themselves an adequate income *when they did work*. Therefore, the programs will provide at best reasonably adequate support in time of need only for those persons with a history of providing themselves—almost exclusively through work efforts—with an adequate income.

Workmen's Compensation[8]

Our earliest income maintenance program was workmen's compensation. These programs were first because industrial accidents were the first and most difficult to ignore of all social risks of industrialization. They were administered by the states and were designed to protect workers against the risks (injury, accident, and death) associated with working on a job. They protect workers exclusively against wage loss caused by on-the-job accidents. Although benefits paid in a given case are specified by state law, much of the insurance from which benefits are paid is sold by private carriers. A worker generally needs only to be employed at the time of the industrial accident to qualify for benefits. The programs provide necessary medical care and vocational rehabilitation in addition to direct cash benefits.

The theory of workmen's compensation is that many industrial accidents are unavoidable. Given this fact, the problem is how those accidents and their associated costs will be compensated. Workmen's compensation assigns the cost of industrial accidents directly to the price of the products produced by the firms in which the accidents occur by legally requiring employers to provide (or pay the premiums for) insurance protection for their employees. In theory, the cost is passed on to the consumer in the price of the products. Society is protected presumably from the possibility that workers who suffer industrial accidents will become dependent for financial support on the general public. Society will be protected to the extent that workmen's compensation benefits replace wages lost because of industrial accidents. Consumption will remain high; and society will benefit from a reasonably uninterrupted high level of economic activity. Individual workers who suffer accidents and their families will be protected against income loss. The provision of medical care and vocational rehabilitation supports the basic protection of the worker and society.

The extent to which the program replaces the lost wages is a measure of its success. The usual evaluation of wage loss replacement compares benefits paid by a given program with some measure of workers' earnings. This approach poses at least two problems in the case of workmen's compensation. First, not all workers are covered, the major exclusions in most state programs being employees of small firms, nonprofit organizations, and agricultural establishments. Although the national average is about 85 percent, the percentage of the total labor force covered ranges from about 40 percent to about 98 percent among the states. It is impossible, of course, to replace the wage loss of an injured worker not covered by the program.

Second, workers who suffer on-the-job injuries are frequently injured on a permanent basis, either totally or partially. Actual wage loss replacement is eventually going to be limited because many states' laws contain limits of liability (effectively limitations on the total dollar amount that will be paid in any individual cases). The data on wage loss replacement can be viewed from several perspectives. For our purposes, two will be used: the percentage of wage loss actually replaced in short-term (six months or less) cases involving total disability; maximum allowable benefits expressed as a percentage of state average weekly earnings; and the percentage of wage loss replaced for widows in case of death. The national average of wage loss replacement is 54 percent, i.e., for every dollar of income lost because of an industrial injury, about 54 cents is replaced for the injured worker and his family. It should be noted that no worker received more than a 40 percent replacement in 20 states (Table 1).

TABLE 1

**Percentage of Wage Loss
Replaced in Temporary Total Disability**

Wage Loss Replaced	State Programs
(percentage)	(number)
60 or more	2
50-59	14
40-49	18
30-39	18
29 or less	2

Source: *Compendium on Workmen's Compensation,* National Commission on Workmen's Compensation Laws (1973).

A similar situation exists in the comparison of state average weekly earnings and maximum allowable benefits. Twenty-four states have legislated maximum replacements of less than 50 percent of wage loss. Widows realize an average of 54 percent of wage loss.

Finally, the program can be considered in terms of whether maximum allowable benefits keep beneficiaries out of poverty. As of January 1972, the programs of 34 states paid maximum allowable benefit amounts that would *not* allow recipients to avoid official classification as impoverished. The National Commission on State Workmen's Compensation Laws (a governmental study group created by the Occupational Health and Safety Act of 1970) evaluated the merit of state programs in this language, "Our intensive evaluation of the evidence compels us to conclude that state workmen's compensation laws are in general neither adequate nor equitable."[9]

Unemployment Insurance

Unemployment insurance came into existence with the Social Security Act of 1935. The major reason for its delay was the failure of Congress to find a mechanism to assure that states would follow the federal example in adoption of such programs. The Social Security Act provided a federal payroll tax with the provision for return of 90 percent of the tax to any state which adopted an unemployment insurance program. Federal law requires employers to be taxed in any case. Within two years, all states had adopted unemployment insurance laws.

The goal of unemployment insurance is protection of workers with histories of substantial labor market attachment who become involuntarily unemployed for a short period through no fault of their own. Originally no state paid benefits for more than 26 weeks. Today several states have 39-week maximums, but the programs are still designed to deal with short-term unemployment.

Unemployment insurance attempts to protect the worker and his or her dependents against wage loss and to maintain consumption at the macro or general economic level. The second goal, protection of society generally, is achieved to precisely the degree that the first goal is. Finally, unemployment insurance has an additional goal which is seldom recognized or understood by the public. It is the attempt to assist the natural workings of the labor market to ensure a maximum or optimal allocation or utilization of manpower resources.[10] Society is presumed to be better off if people are employed and doing those things for which they are best prepared and able, i.e., utilizing fully their skills, training, education, etc. One of the less apparent social costs of unemployment is the forcing of workers to accept jobs which fail to utilize fully their abilities. To the extent that unemployment insurance benefits allow unemployed workers to maintain their expenditure patterns, those workers are not forced to accept jobs that represent a misuse of their skills and capacities.

In contrast to workmen's compensation, workers must not only be covered by the law but must become unemployed for the "correct" reasons under employment insurance because the law is designed only to protect "involuntarily" unemployed workers. Virtually all states identify causes of unemployment deemed inappropriate to benefit payments. These circumstances, usually called "disqualifications," include generally the following: voluntarily quitting or leaving work, misconduct connected with work, refusal of suitable job offers, unemployment connected with a labor dispute, fraudulent misrepresentation, and receipt of other income.[11]

In general, the effectiveness of the unemployment insurance program is measured by the extent to which lost wages are replaced. The current situation in wage loss replacement, or what is called "benefit adequacy," is depicted below (Table 2). The table indicates that at best few programs would replace more than 70 percent of wage loss if the statutory goals were met. The performance of unemployment insurance is below even its modest target. In terms of its three program objectives, the unemployment insurance program appears to be a substantial failure.

TABLE 2

Distribution of State Unemployment Insurance
Programs by Percentage of Actual Wage Loss Replaced
by Benefits

Wage Loss Replacement	Numbers of States [1]	
	Statutory Goal	Actual Replacement
(percentage)		
80 or more	6	0
70-79	0	0
60-69	10	0
50-59	36	9
40-49	0	25
30-39	0	18

Source: *Social Security Programs in the United States* (1972)
[1] including District of Columbia and Puerto Rico

Old Age, Survivors, Disability, and Health Insurance

Like unemployment insurance, OASDHI is a product of the 1930s depression. OASDHI is the major institutionalized method in this nation for protecting workers and their families from significant income loss from retirement, premature death, permanent and total disability, and the medical expense of old age. In December 1974, this combined program paid benefits of $5 billion to over 31 million persons. An indication of the importance of OASDHI is that only 2 million persons received state unemployment benefits in the same month.

OASDHI has attempted from its beginning to protect persons against income loss if these persons had substantial records of productive employment. It does not and cannot protect persons without a history of being able to protect themselves. A worker's entitlement to benefits and his benefit amount reflect his past earnings in covered employment.

Benefits under this program are an earned right. They are paid regardless of the worker's receipt of income from nonwork sources, dividends, real estate, etc. Unlike both unemployment insurance and workmen's compensation, workers make direct contributions to their insurance, usually one-half of the cost. This fact emphasizes the principle of benefits as a legal right. The contributory nature of the program encourages worker interest in and responsiveness to the program and changes in it.

TABLE 3

OASDHI Benefits and Beneficiaries
December 1974

Reason for Entitlement	Amount of Benefits	Number Beneficiaries
	(millions)	(millions)
Retirement	$3273	19.7
Disability	557	3.9
Survivor	8	7.2
Medical care	1162	.4

Source: *Social Security Bulletin,* April 1975

    OASDHI coverage is compulsory to the extent possible under the Constitution. Both the financial soundness and economic effectiveness of the program would be threatened in the absence of such compulsion. There would be a strong tendency for poorer risks to participate, and for better risks to invest elsewhere with a resulting significant increase in program costs and contribution rates. This principle of compulsion is often misunderstood. The simple fact is that without its presence OASDHI would cease to exist.

    Finally, OASDHI benefit rights—the amount of benefits and the circumstances under which they will be paid—are defined clearly and related generally to facts that can be determined objectively. There is little opportunity for administrative discretion; a person meeting the legal conditions must be paid or he or she may exercise the right of a direct appeal to the federal court.

    OASDHI represents by a significant margin the largest single income maintenance program in the U.S. The discontinuance of OASDHI benefits would create more poor people than any other single action. The significance of the program decreases somewhat when the question of benefit adequacy is considered. Although many approaches are available to assess benefit adequacy, the extent to which benefits enable recipients to maintain a reasonable (but minimal) level of existence is employed here. The budget figures are those prepared by the Bureau of Labor Statistics for support at a "modest but adequate living standard." If one compares average OASDHI benefits with the cost of this budget beginning in 1948, benefits fail to cover the cost. One major reason is the differential impact of inflation on older persons. The concentration of inflation on items like food, clothing, and medical care has assured a disproportionately greater impact on older persons. The advent of OASDHI medical insurance has helped, but not solved, the problem.

Although OASDHI has failed to solve some of the problems and meet some of the goals that many feel it might have achieved in income maintenance, the program remains the most powerful income security device in the U.S.

Public Assistance

The final set of programs in the traditional income maintenance structure is public assistance, popularly called "welfare." These programs are well-defined in terms of the population they seek to assist, are administered by states (often through counties), and are financed jointly by federal and state governments. In contrast to the three programs reviewed above, all public assistance programs (PAP) require that claimants establish their economic need. These standards of need are usually in the form of a subsistence budget and are administered rigorously.

TABLE 4

Selected Data on Public Assistance Programs
July 1973

Program	Number of Beneficiaries	Average Monthly Payment
	(thousands)	
Old age assistance	1,839	$ 78.80
Aid to the blind	78	111.25
Aid to disabled	1,217	109.90
Aid to families with dependent children	10,852	187.30
General assistance	746	72.95

Source: *Social Security Bulletin,* December 1973.

The PAP are designed to assist individuals in several categories as the program titles indicate. Old-Age Assistance, Aid to the Blind, Aid to the Permanently and Totally Disabled, and Aid to Families with Dependent Children. The specific beneficiary designation may reflect their attachment to the notion of the "worthy poor"—"safe bets" for public financial support.

Most states have one additional program, usually called General Assistance, designed to offer support for those who qualify on a need basis but are not in any of the first four categories. The general assistance program is of considerable significance but is next to the smallest of the various programs.

Although some of these programs have large numbers of recipients, the benefits per recipient are quite small. As is true with workmen's compensation and unemployment insurance and (to a lesser extent) OASDHI, although low benefits are preferable to no benefits, these programs can hardly be considered major assaults on the problems of poverty in this nation.

THE WAR ON POVERTY

Official recognition of the existence of poverty in the U.S. occurred when the 1964 *Economic Report of the President* noted that[12]

> ... in his message on the State of the Union, President Johnson declared all-out war on poverty in America ... the overriding objective is to improve the quality of life of individual human beings. For poverty deprives the individual not of material comforts but of human dignity and fulfillment. Poverty is rarely a builder of character.

The problem attacked was indeed significant. The same report estimated that 30 million persons, representing about 20 percent of our population, were poor. The definition used to separate the poor from the nonpoor was the now-famous $3,000 annual income for a family of four persons.

The "war" declared by Lyndon Johnson consisted of a (hopefully) coordinated series of specific attacks on poverty. In the variety of specific programs there was a strong attempt to recognize the complex and cyclical nature of poverty. Poverty was characterized in the report in these terms:[13]

> Poverty breeds poverty. A poor individual or family has a high probability of remaining poor. Low incomes carry with them high risks of illness; limitation on mobility; limited access to education, information, and training. Poor parents cannot give their children the opportunities for better health and education needed to improve their lot. Lack of motivation, hope and incentive is a more subtle but no less powerful barrier than lack of financial means. Thus the cruel legacy of poverty is passed from parent to children.

Pursuing this brief analysis of the multifaceted nature of poverty, the Congress at President Johnson's urging passed the Economic Opportunity Act (EOA) of 1964. This legislation, known popularly as the antipoverty bill, represented a pluralistic attack on the problem of domestic poverty.

Its initial funding was $963 million. To place this funding in perspective, the student is reminded that our nation was spending $30 billion per year in Vietnam at the peak of our involvement. The point is not whether this nation should have been involved in Vietnam but rather to emphasize the relatively modest expenditures for our "war" on poverty. Total funding for the various poverty programs for the years 1965-1967 was less than $4 billion.

Specific Programs

Many of the specific programs of the War on Poverty represented efforts to attack poverty among young persons. The programs recognized the "cyclical" nature of poverty and attempted to break into the cycle at the lower end of the age distribution. Title I of the EOA established three separate programs for young persons. The Job Corps was to assist young persons from poor families with preparation for responsible citizenship and economic roles by providing rural and urban vocational training centers and youth conservation camps. An allied effort was the Work-Training and Work-Study program. Both assisted young persons in remaining in school while earning an income. The former was for high school students and the latter for college students. The federal government paid 90 percent of the costs, and the student's employer the remaining 10 percent.

The Community Action Program was designed to stimulate rural and urban communities to assemble resources to combat poverty. This section of the EOA attempted to encourage these communities to identify, define, and develop solutions to local poverty problems. Examples of programs developed are local job training and counseling, child dental care, home management and legal aid for the poor, Montessori education for poverty youngsters, baby-sitting services for working mothers, and preschool programs for young children. Funds for these programs were granted directly to local Community Action Commissions by the Office of Economic Opportunity which administered the EOA. An additional effort in this direction was the Adult Basic Education Program which provided support to local programs designed to increase the literacy level of persons 18 years or older who were handicapped vocationally by their limited ability to read and write. Finally, the Voluntary Assistance Program provided an institutional mechanism by which adults could offer partial financial support for needy children on a regular basis.

In addition to local community programs, the EOA offered long-term, low-interest loans for farmers and businessmen to expand and modernize their business facilities in order to increase local employment opportunities. Title V provided funds for experimental projects to increase the number of employables able to care for themselves and support their families. Finally, the EOA established a "domestic Peace Corps," Volunteers in Service to America or VISTA. The VISTA participants received monthly maintenance allowances and were assigned to work in various poverty programs and projects.

This brief review of specific EOA programs and their wide variety points, among other things, to the really modest amounts of money that were spent in funding this "war."

Poverty, Progress, and Income Maintenance

We turn now to the results of both the War on Poverty and traditional income maintenance programs reviewed above. Our analysis considers the overall impact of these efforts on the poverty group in society. The relevant question is simply, "Did these programs alleviate or eliminate poverty?" Is the poverty situation any better now than it was when poverty was discovered as a political reality in 1964? Two criteria are used in seeking the answer. First, are there fewer poor people now than prior to the initiation of the programs. Second, has the composition of the poverty group changed? The data yield several important conclusions (Table 5). The total number of poor persons has decreased

TABLE 5

Selected Data on Persons in Poverty, 1959-1972

Characteristics	Year				
	1959	*1966*	*1969*	*1971*	*1972*
			(thousands)		
Number of Poor Persons	*39,490*	*28,510*	*24,147*	*25,559*	*24,460*
Poor persons as percentage of all persons in given group			*(percentages)*		
All persons	22.4	14.7	12.1	12.5	11.9
Age 65 and over	n.a.	28.5	n.a.	21.6	18.6
Unrelated persons	46.1	38.3	34.0	31.6	29.0
Persons in families headed by a male:					
White	14.7	8.0	6.0	6.2	5.6
Nonwhite	51.0	31.2	19.8	19.1	18.5
Persons in families headed by a female:					
White	41.2	29.7	29.1	30.4	27.4
Nonwhite	75.6	64.6	57.8	55.6	57.7

n.a.—not available
Source: *Economic Report of the President,* 1974.

substantially, particularly among white and nonwhite families headed by males. However, the reason probably has little to do with the antipoverty programs. The 1974 *Economic Report of the President* argues rather persuasively that:[14]

> The principal factor behind the decline in poverty is economic growth. The basic forces underlying economic growth have raised the production of even the least skilled worker and have enabled millions of workers to rise above the low-income threshold through a higher wage role in the labor force. In addition, economic growth has increased the labor force participation of wives by increasing their labor market wage rate . . . the decline in poverty has been most pronounced for the working poor . . . Those levels of families who do not work but are no longer in poverty have benefited from increases in social security and pension income, which were made possible by economic growth.

The remaining poor persons are increasingly in situations which make the possibility of their working remote. On balance, although progress has occurred, two observations seem pertinent. First, the total number of poor who remain in our nation is large. Second, the impact of poverty on various subcultures within society remains widely different. The second observation may eventually become the more important to U.S. society.

GUARANTEED INCOME AND
NATIONAL MINIMUM PROPOSALS

With increased interest in poverty, many proposals have received public attention and some serious public support. These proposals may be grouped into two general categories: those attempting to achieve an income guarantee and those attempting to deal exclusively with the poverty problems of children. The guaranteed income proposals vary widely in content, mechanics, and income to be guaranteed. However, they have one common characteristic, a commitment to the principle of a guarantee. Some of the proposals include, as a balance, the phasing out of current welfare programs. Although it has received substantial attention, the so-called negative income tax proposal does not differ in principle from the guaranteed income schemes. The concept behind all of these proposals is that society should guarantee all citizens a minimum cash income because they are citizens. The amount varies, of course, with the goal of the proposal. Most of the dollar amounts proposed have been related to some notion of a minimum but adequate standard of living (usually emphasizing the minimum aspect).

The second category of current proposals is typified by a variety of family allowance proposals that have been advanced.[15] The suggested programs are more narrow in scope and attempt to assure that children will receive minimum living standards of food, clothing, shelter, medical care, and education.

Their conceptual basis is that the children are citizens and that they are children. Although the idea of income guarantees is hardly universal, most industrialized nations except the U.S. have a family allowance program.

Although not currently an active proposal, there is the idea of a "national minimum." This concept is a legislated fact in Great Britain and certain other western European nations and argues that all citizens, because they are citizens, have a right to a minimum life experience. In practice, this minimum includes food, housing, clothing, education, employment, medical care, and related items, and is achieved through many programs. These programs are financed invariably from the general national tax revenues. Although such a proposal is not current in the U.S., it may become the agreed target for public policy in a tomorrow not far away.

CONCLUSION

We have examined the historical and contemporary contexts of economic insecurity. Traditional and recent approaches to the problem were considered. Although progress in the reduction of poverty has occurred in the last decade, additional emphasis and programs are required if the U.S. is to achieve a reasonable income distribution. The coming years will undoubtedly see additional initiatives toward this end.

IMPORTANT NEW TERMS INTRODUCED

Poverty: The politically defined standard of living below which people generally are considered to be significantly disadvantaged.

Income maintenance programs: The collection of public and private schemes designed to protect workers and their families against conventional industrial risks, i.e., old age, unemployment, and industrial injury.

Guaranteed income: A series of differing specific proposals, all of which attempt to assure individuals and families, whether working or not, minimum amounts of cash income.

SUGGESTED ADDITIONAL READINGS

Michael Harrington, *The Other America: Poverty in the United States* (Baltimore: Penguin Books, 1963).

Frances Fox Piven and Richard A. Cowen, *Regulating the Poor: The Functions of Public Welfare* (New York: Random House, 1971).

William Ryan, *Blaming the Victim* (New York: Random House, 1971).

Bradley R. Schiller, *The Economics of Poverty and Discrimination* (Englewood Cliffs: Prentice-Hall, 1973).

NOTES

[1] For example, one of the classic explanations for the emergence of poverty in western industrialized nations includes a thorough analysis of industrialization and urbanization, the enclosure movement in Britain and France, and allied occurrences.

[2] The student interested in a general analysis of the significance of matching specific problems and solutions is referred to Nathan Glazer, "The Limits of Social Policy," *Commentary* (September 1971), pp. 51-58.

[3] Kark de Schweinitz, *England's Road to Social Security* (New York: A. S. Barnes, 1962) contains detailed analysis of the historical development of these programs.

[4] William Ryan, *Blaming the Victim* (New York: Vintage Books, 1971) has a complete account of the negative aspects.

[5] There has always been a large difference in the U.S. between the operation of income maintenance programs and *any* attempt to combat poverty. The programs attempted to insure people against the loss of income when that loss could be traced directly to the occurrence of a specific risk.

[6] A popular manifestation of this viewpoint was the emergence in the 1960s of an automobile bumper-sticker that contained the message, "I fight poverty, I work."

[7] The student interested in a more general analysis of this question of whether poor people have different value structures from the nonpoor is referred to Hyman Rodman, "The Lower Class Value Stretch," *Social Forces* (December 1963), pp. 205-215.

[8] The student can obtain a detailed description of these programs in Herman M. and Anne R. Somers, *Workmen's Compensation* (New York: John Wiley, 1954).

[9] *Report of the National Commission of State Workmen's Compensation Laws* (Washington: U.S. Government Printing Office, 1972), pp. 24-25.

[10] This subject is discussed in greater detail in Chapter 4.

[11] See Ralph Altman, *Availability for Work: A Study of Unemployment Compensation* (Cambridge: Harvard University Press, 1950), and Fred Slavick, *Voluntary Quit Disqualification in Unemployment Insurance— The Iowa Experience* (Iowa City: Bureau of Labor and Management, 1958).

[12] *Economic Report of the President* (Washington: U.S. Government Printing Office, 1964), p. 55.

[13] Ibid., pp. 69-70.

[14] *Economic Report of the President* (Washington: U.S. Government Printing Office, 1974), pp. 162-163.

[15] See James C. Vadakin, *Children, Poverty, and Family Allowances* (New York: Basic Books, 1968).

4

Government Regulation of the Labor Market

INTRODUCTION

The labor market, its organization, and the way it functions are very important in American society because of the reliance placed on the relationship of work to income. The source of income for virtually all Americans who receive any substantial amount is work as defined in the traditional labor market context. We discussed the organization of the labor market in Chapter 2 and indicated what that organization should do with respect to setting wage rates and allocating scarce resources. The preceding chapter on poverty suggested, among other things, that this labor market organization apparently does not function as it is supposed to, particularly in terms of distributing income.

Presumably one of the responsibilities of government in a free society is to intervene when the functioning of the market is not resulting in the kind of relationships which society expected when that market was established. For example, during periods of national emergency (e.g., wars) governments have invariably intervened to control otherwise free markets. This chapter portrays some of the more significant occasions on which government has intervened in the operation of the labor market. In each case, an attempt is made to describe briefly the intervention and the goal sought and to provide some evaluation of its success. Throughout this chapter, the student should remember that our society's legal sanction of labor organizations probably represents in the final analysis the single most important example of government regulation of labor markets. The effects of labor organizations are not considered in this chapter, but we do consider three instances of government regulation of the labor market: minimum wages; equal employment opportunities; and the U.S. Employment (or Manpower) Service.

FAIR LABOR STANDARDS ACT

Minimum wage and maximum hours legislation in the United States is almost 40 years old. Both the federal and most state governments have set some standard *minimum wage* below which no person covered by the legislation can be employed legally, and have placed some premium on hours over 40 worked in any single week. Minimum wage laws are an attempt to achieve several compatible goals: establishment of a wage rate below which no one will have to work; promotion of a higher national product by increasing consumption expenditures through increased wage rates; and increased employment by increasing the costs of overtime.

Minimum wage laws make one very important assumption in the pursuit of these goals, i.e., employers who, prior to legislation, had paid hourly wages below the stated minimum are capable of paying at least the minimum. Obviously this assumption is extremely important because if it is not true, enactment of a minimum will cause widespread unemployment rather than achieve the presumably desirable goal.

We must consider the theoretical argument in order to assess the apparent impact of minimum wages. Conventional economic theory argues that any market for a product or a factor of production will create a stable price within a reasonable period of operation. This price will equate the supply of and demand for whatever is being traded in the market and all will presumably be well. From the viewpoint of conventional theory, minimum wage legislation artificially increases the market price and should reduce employment. This argument has been the historic basis of much of the opposition to minimum wage laws and can be depicted graphically in the following terms (Fig. 1). The figure assumes an imaginary economy with two sectors—A and B. The two

FIGURE 1

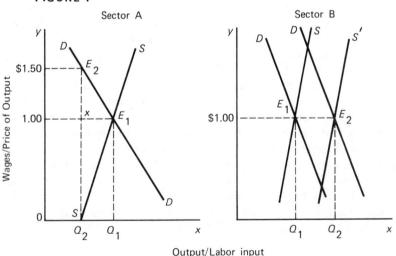

Output/Labor input

sectors are initially both in a condition of equilibrium. The prices of both labor inputs and products of the sectors are assumed to be be the same. All of the assumptions are made out of a concern for analytic simplicity. The presence or absence of any of the assumptions does not affect the basic value of the analysis or its conclusions. Sector A is subjected to a legislated minimum wage which increases the market wage from $1 to $1.50. As a result of the increase in labor costs, the demand for labor in Sector A is reduced from Q_1 to Q_2. At the same time, the price of the product in Sector A increases because of increased labor costs and the demand for the product decreases. As a result, the demand for the products of Sector B and the demand for labor and other productive factors in Sector B will increase. This increase is depicted by the shifts in the demand and supply schedules for Sector B and the increase, in particular, in labor inputs used in Sector B from Q_1 to Q_2. The problem is stated here in the most optimistic terms in that the total resources forced out of Sector A by the advent of the minimum wage are totally absorbed in Sector B, i.e., no unemployment is caused by the increase in the cost of labor in Sector A. Alternative assumptions, of course, would cause the level of unemployment "caused" by the minimum to increase and to eventually represent all of the resources which are released by Sector A following the advent of the minimum wage. However, regardless of the level of unemployment in the theory, one major difficulty remains in terms of conventional economic theory. The minimum wage has caused a resource misallocation. The resources represented in Fig. 1 by the rectangle $Q_1, Q_2 XE_1$ (Sector A) have been forced into Sector B when, in conventional theoretical terms, they "belong" in Sector A. J. R. Hicks, the noted British economist, put the problem well when he noted that:[1]

> In this case, it is not the unemployment which is, economically speaking, the most significant effect of regulation (in an extreme case, where the affected firms are abnormally prosperous, and the rise in wages is only just sufficient to prevent their expanding employment or to diminish their expansion, there may be no net unemployment due to the regulation); the important effect is the redistribution of labor—the fact that some men are prevented from securing employment in a trade where they would be better off than they are otherwise condemned to be.

The data regarding the impact of minimum wage legislation which is used here represent studies and analysis which relate exclusively to the Fair Labor Standards Act (FLSA). Beginning with the initial minimums in the late 1930s the Department of Labor has consistently studied the impact of the FLSA in terms of employment.[2] In addition to the work done by the Department of Labor, academicians have independently analyzed various types of minimum wage impact.[3] A similar conclusion emerges from all of these studies, regardless of source. The FLSA appears not to cause the negative impacts of unemployment that conventional theory indicates. The data strongly indicate that managements were paying workers initially less than they could afford. R. A. Lester summarized the conclusions of most studies when he stated:[4]

> Despite the limitations of the data and the difficulties of reading cause and effect relationships into statistics, some conclusions can be drawn from minimum wage experience. The studies show that there is not a consistent and compelling relationship between minimum wage increases and changes in employment in the affected plants. That, however, is a negative conclusion. It does not provide positive proof for an alternative explanation of other relationships. Some of the evidence does seem to support a conclusion that even in relatively small low-wage firms, managements have some latitude of adjustment and can, therefore, adapt a new minimum in a variety of ways, including better utilization of labor and efforts to improve the work force.

Therefore, we may conclude that minimum wage legislation has been identifiably, although not completely, successful in achieving its goals.

EQUAL EMPLOYMENT OPPORTUNITY LEGISLATION

As with minimum wage legislation, equal employment opportunity legislation exists at both federal and state levels. A number of municipal laws actually preceded federal and state laws. Although the Civil Rights Act of 1964 has tended to occupy public attention in recent years, state and city fair employment practices legislation dates back to the immediate post-World War II period. For example, some 37 states had some form of fair employment practices legislation at the time of the passage of the 1964 federal legislation. In addition to state and local efforts, the federal government had a long history, dating from the post-World War II period, of enforcing rigorously both as an employer and as a contractor for goods and services the notion of nondiscrimination. The President's Commission on Government Contracts has long served as an effective watchdog on compliance with general guidelines of nondiscrimination by employers doing work under government contract.

The goal of all fair employment practices legislation is twofold: to prohibit discrimination in order to make effective the guarantees in the federal Constitution of equality for all citizens, and to attempt to avoid the undesirable inequities in economic opportunity and achievement which discriminatory practices invariably cause. The reader need only recall from our earlier discussion of poverty the fact that at any given level of education a black citizen's chance of being poor is approximately twice that of his white counterpart to appreciate the economic significance of discrimination. So much of income attainment depends directly on employment possibilities of people that the importance of equal employment practices should be obvious.

The major federal legislation on this subject is the Civil Rights Act of 1964. Its goal is to effectively end discrimination in the labor market. The Act established the Equal Employment Opportunity Commission (EEOC) as the major enforcer of public policy with relatively broad powers. The EEOC is charged with enforcement in regard to hiring and firing practices, wages, working conditions, promotion, and other personnel policies of employers, unions, employment agencies, state and local governments, educational institutions, and training agents. Under the law, persons may not be discriminated against because of race, religion, national origin, or sex.

It is important to realize that for the first eight years of the existence of the EEOC its activities were substantially limited to investigation, conciliation, and persuasion. Although legislation to broaden EEOC power to include the ability to seek cease-and-desist orders from the federal courts was introduced in the Congress each year after passage of the basic law in 1964, it was not until March 1972 that EEOC acquired this power.[5] Acquisition of this authority carried forward the general tone of antidiscrimination legislation. The purpose of such legislation is to encourage people to behave in a generally acceptable or reasonable fashion rather than to punish them. Therefore, the emphasis in the enforcement procedure in such legislation is on techniques of persuasion and conciliation.

However, the effectiveness of EEOC remains considerably weakened by the legal requirement that it become involved in cases only after a formal complaint is filed by a person who thinks that he or she has been the object of discrimination. Then, even if the charge proves correct, no real sanctions can be imposed by EEOC nor does EEOC undertake publication of the fact that the offending party has engaged in an act of discrimination. The fact that EEOC is dependent upon the filing of a formal complaint before it can take any action has many weaknesses. First, it is expensive and time-consuming to work through each complaint filed with the agency. For example, EEOC succeeded in completing work on only 300 cases from 1963 to 1966. Second, the aggrieved party has little incentive to file a complaint. Given the available enforcement powers, the direct complaint procedure results frequently in union or employer retaliation, although it may produce a promotion, wage increase, or employment. The difficulty is that the procedure places nearly all of the burden for achievement of equality on the individual worker.

Despite these weaknesses, the Nixon administration pursued vigorously one area in which the removal of discriminatory practice appears to have substantial promise and economic rewards for minority persons. Beginning in 1966, the Department of Labor advanced a program to improve the status of black workers in the construction industry. The specific target of this attempt, which has become known popularly as the "Philadelphia Plan," was an increase in the proportion of new black entrants into the building trades to 5 percent in 1970 and to 25 percent in 1975. These efforts have generally been evaluated as substantial failures.[6] This lack of success is particularly discouraging because the federal government should be able to use the force of its legislative mandate and its role as a purchaser of the product in the construction industry. By the late 1960s and early 1970s, at least one-third of the total output of the industry was purchased with federal funds.

However, one must recognize both the difficulty of the task and the political power of the building trades unions. As we shall see in Chapter 5, these unions are very well established and very conservative. The failure of efforts like the "Philadelphia Plan" was predictable. History may eventually judge this experience as a somewhat reluctant beginning rather than a total failure.

One must realize also that the activities of EEOC do not represent the total effort for combatting employment discrimination. At the federal level, there is a successor agency to the aforementioned President's Commission on Government Contracts, the Office of Federal Contract Compliance (OFCC). Unlike EEOC, OFCC has relatively strong investigative and enforcement powers. OFCC can initiate investigations, impose sanctions, and cause government contracts to be terminated prematurely in those situations in which substantial discrimination exists. OFCC can require employers to institute "affirmative action" (invoke policies actively favoring minority persons) in order to balance previous discriminations. The scope of OFCC authority applies to all businesses that sell or service products to or for the federal government. In 1972, over one-third of our total labor force was subject to the activities of the OFCC. Although there has been some evidence that the program has been hindered by elected officials, it generally appears to be successfully operated.

In addition to the recognition of multiple approaches to the problem, there are alternative means for evaluating the degree of success in reducing employment discrimination. It is appropriate to end our discussion of equal employment opportunity legislation with a brief review of two approaches. Women and blacks represent two groups on whose behalf major efforts have been expended over the past several years. A consideration of their progress follows.

We must remember that there are many forces that promote a reduction of employment discrimination. Therefore, it would be misleading to suggest that such reduction is due only to the 1964 legislation or any other specific event. The ratios in Table 1 represent the result of dividing the indicated value (e.g., median income) for nonwhites by the comparable value for whites. An increase in resulting value indicates progress for the group. The data indicate progress over both 10-year periods. The progress is particularly notable between 1960 and 1970 and for black women. Other data indicate similar progress. For example, the percentage of black college graduates holding managerial positions

TABLE 1

Selected Changes in the Ratios
of White and Nonwhite Economic Positions

Ratio or basis for comparison	1950	1960	1970
		Years	
		(percentages)	
Median income (females)	.50	.57	.86
Median income (males)	.56	.58	.64
Median income (males aged 20-24)	.68	.67	.82
Occupational index (male)	.76	.79	.87
Occupational index (female)	.49	.66	.85
Income (male college graduates)	.60	.65	.73
Income (female college graduates)	.91	.99	1.25
Income (professional males)	.57	.68	.72
Income (professional females)	.85	.97	1.18

Source: Richard B. Freeman, "Decline of Labor Market Discrimination and Economic Analysis," *American Economic Review,* 63, No. 2 (May 1973), p. 281.

increased from 7 percent in 1960 to 13 percent in 1970. Although all of these data are encouraging, it remains evident that much is left before accomplishing the goal of a labor market which will not discriminate against nonwhites.

A picture of substantial progress also exists in terms of women's position in the labor market. In both quantitative and qualitative terms, the situation of women has advanced signifcantly during the past decade. Although this progress can be attributed to the Civil Rights Act, much of the credit is due to private organizations and pressure groups. In 1972, 30 percent of the formal complaints received by EEOC and the majority of actions brought under the Equal Pay Act of 1963 involved alleged discrimination against women.

UNITED STATES EMPLOYMENT SERVICE

Perhaps the outstanding characteristic of the U.S. labor market is its disorganization. The theoretical model of the labor market described in most introductory economics textbooks assumes the labor market is a rational place where unemployed workers look systematically for work, primarily through public employment exchanges; and where employers with job vacancies utilize similar search patterns. The passage of the Wagner-Psyer Act of 1932 created the U.S. Employment Service (ES). The agency goal was establishment of the orderly labor market envisioned in the textbooks through federal-state cooperation. Unfortunately, neither workers nor employers have utilized ES facilities. In one sense, this nonutilization is irrational, particularly by employers because the ES is financed directly by a tax on their payrolls. Employers have already paid for a labor market service which they generally ignore.

Many employers have argued that they do not use the ES because workers do not use it. Workers fail to use the ES because they are convinced that employers do not utilize it. It is clear that the worker's preference is for what is normally referred to as "informal methods" of seeking work. These refer to search patterns that focus on employer gate applications and "leads" furnished by personal acquaintances. The preference for this approach has been confirmed by nearly all labor market studies in the U.S. This preference is shown in the following table from an early post-World War II study. Although either use of the ES or newspaper advertisements would represent the more rational alternatives, worker preference is not for them. One reason for the "poor press" of the ES is the employer belief that the ES will supply disproportionate numbers of dissatisfied persons or "floaters" who will prove to be a disruptive influence in the company.[7] Other research indicates that workers fail to use the ES either because they believe it has few, if any, worthwhile jobs or because they feel that its clients are substantially inferior.[8] There are two, more subjective, barriers to ES use, revealed by recent research. First, except for the unskilled, most workers perceive no ES relevance to them. Second, many workers (particularly white-collar workers) have a substantial (albeit unconscious) unwillingness to admit that they need help in finding work.[9] These facts and attitudes indicate that the ES is not going to be able to perform its presumed function of helping to rationalize the U.S. labor market without substantial modification of both employers' and workers' attitudes.

Many observers note the activities of the Wisconsin ES in the Madison

TABLE 2

**Percentage Distribution of Manual Workers
by Method of Learning About Present Job**

Method	Percentage
Acquaintances or relatives: working in plant	24
Acquaintances or relatives: not in plant	4
Direct application at plant	20
Returning to plant where previously worked	13
State employment service	13
Advertisements	13
Union	5
Other	8

Source: Table 16 "Method of Learning About Present Job," in *The Structure of Labor Markets* by Lloyd G. Reynolds (Harper and Row, 1951), p. 106.

market during the early 1960s as a good example of the type of success that the ES can have. However, they recognize and agree that the Madison experience was unique in many respects. First, the ES was the dominant force in the labor market, i.e., other institutional forces (unions, private employment agencies, etc.) were absent. Second, the Madison labor market possessed some unique characteristics, including a very high clerical worker turnover, which the ES was able to utilize. Finally, the ES was able by careful management of the situation to overcome the usual worker and employer prejudice against its use and thereby structure a local labor market, at least for clerical workers, in which both workers and firms could make reasonable decisions.[10] Thus, under certain circumstances, the ES can succeed in its goal of labor market rationalization.

Despite this instance of success, the ES remains a generally ineffective force. In the latter half of the 1960s, the Secretary of Labor appointed a special high-level task force to answer the question, "What is needed to make the ES a significant force in the labor market?" The task force surveyed chief administrators of the state ES agencies. These administrators agreed generally that the following changes were necessary: a new and stronger legislative mandate; higher salaries for state agency employees; permission to shift employees among various state and federal ES offices; a national job and worker clearinghouse; compulsory job vacancy listings by the government and government contractors; and authority for state agencies to contract with nongovernmental organizations for specialized manpower services.[11]

Many of the task force recommendations were implemented, but the overall effectiveness of the ES has changed little except for its activities on behalf of government employees. The poor performance has become more disturbing in the past six to eight years as additional federal legislation—the Civil Rights Act, Public Works and Economic Development Act, Model Cities legislation, etc.—has extended new responsibilities, authority, and funding to the ES. Between 1962 and 1972, ES federal funding increased from $147 million to $379 million, but its nonfarm placements decreased from 6.5 million to 3.8 million. The ES has consistently been able to do less with more funds. President Nixon noted in the 1973 *Manpower Report* that[12]

> Severe inflation near the end of the decade and the economic downturn of 1970 led many to look again to the ES as a labor exchange merchanism. But the employment service was by then unable to serve very effectively either the job-ready or the disadvantaged with their need for employability development.

Therefore, the federal efforts to intercede in and regulate the labor market in this very important task of finding jobs for the unemployed and applicants for vacancies has not succeeded. Apparently, until and unless something is done to virtually force workers and employers to use ES facilities, it will remain a failure.

CONCLUSIONS

We have reviewed several distinctly different government efforts to regulate the labor market. The success of the programs is, on balance, as varied as the contents of the programs. One fact emerges. Given the cooperation of the private parties involved and a reasonably strong legislative mandate, governmental regulation in this area can be successful. This is important because it is important for the U.S. public to remember that the results of economic disorganization do not have to be accepted as the natural result of a relatively free economic system. Instead the problems can be met successfully.

IMPORTANT NEW TERMS INTRODUCED

Minimum wage: The lowest wage rate allowed in the United States by either federal or state law.

Fair employment practices legislation: A network of federal and state laws and regulations which prohibit any form of discrimination based on race, religion, creed, ethnic background, age, or sex.

United States Employment Service: A system of employment offices financed primarily by the federal government, which provide a variety of counselling and job referral services.

SUGGESTED ADDITIONAL READINGS

Carroll L. Christenson and Richard A. Mayren, *Wage Policy Under the Walsh-Healey Public Contracts Act: A Critical Review* (Bloomington: Indiana University Press, 1966).

N. Arnold Tolles, "American Minimum Wage Laws: Their Purposes and Effects," *Proceedings of the Twelfth Annual Meeting, Industrial Relations Research Association* (Madison: Industrial Relations Research Association, 1959).

Lloyd Ulman (ed.), *Manpower Programs in the Policy Mix* (Baltimore: The Johns Hopkins University Press, 1973).

NOTES

[1] J. R. Hicks, *The Theory of Wages*, 2nd ed. (London: The Macmillan Co., 1964), p. 180.

[2] Examples of the earliest of these studies include: H. H. Douty, "Minimum Wage Legislation in the Seamless Hosiery Industry," *Southern Economic Journal*, 8, No. 2 (October 1941), p. 176, and, A. F. Hendricks, "Effects of the 25 Cent Minimum Wage on Employment in the Seamless Hosiery Industry," *Journal of the American Statistical Association*, 35, No. 2 (March 1940), p. 13.

[3] See, for example: J. F. Moloney, "Some Effects of the Federal Fair Labor Standards Act upon Southern Industry," *Southern Economic Journal,* 9, No. 3 (July 1942), pp. 15-23; John Peterson, "Employment Effects of Minimum Wage 1938-1950," *Journal of Political Economy,* 65, No. 5 (October 1957), p. 429; Richard A. Lester, "Employment Effects of Minimum Wages: A Communication," *Industrial and Labor Relations Review,* 13, No. 2 (January 1960), pp. 254-64; Marshall R. Colberg, "Agriculture and the Minimum Wage," *Mississippi Valley Journal of Business and Economics,* 3, No. 2 (January 1969), pp. 15-25; and Yale Brozen, "Minimum Wage Rates and Household Workers," *The Journal of Law and Economics,* 5 (October 1962), pp. 103-110.

[4] Richard A. Lester, *The Economics of Labor,* 2nd ed. (New York: The Macmillan Co., 1964), p. 526.

[5] Such orders represent only a legal notice from a court to an offender, identifying the behavior to be stopped. The individual can be cited for failure to stop the behavior and punished. These court orders are generally an effective method of enforcement.

[6] An excellent evaluation of this approach is Benjamin W. Walkinson, "The Effectiveness of EEOC Policy in the Construction Industry," *Annual Proceedings of the Industrial Relations Research Association* (Madison: Industrial Relations Research Association, 1973), pp. 362-369.

[7] E. Wight Bakke and William Noland, *Workers Wanted* (New York: Harper and Row, 1949), p. 138.

[8] For example, see Charles A. Myers, "Labor Mobilities in the Two Communities," *Labor Mobility and Economic Opportunity* (New York: John Wiley, 1954), pp. 77.

[9] Glenn Miller, Frederick A. Zeller, and Robert Miller, "Some Factors Affecting the Role of the Employment Service," *Labor Law Journal,* 16, No. 4 (April 1965), p. 209.

[10] A complete report on this experience is in Eaton H. Conant, "Public Employment Service Operations in a Clerical Labor Market," *Proceedings of the Fifteenth Annual Meeting* (Madison: Industrial Relations Research Association, 1962), pp. 306-314.

[11] Herbert S. Parnes, "The Employment Service Task Force Report," *Proceedings of the Nineteenth Annual Meeting* (Madison: Industrial Relations Research Association, 1966), p. 43.

[12] *Manpower Report of the President 1973* (Washington: U.S. Government Printing Office, 1973), p. 47.

5

American Unions: Their Historical Development

INTRODUCTION

Institutions are studied from a historical viewpoint for many reasons. One may be interested in the history per se. The history of one institution may be studied in order to provide insight and understanding into related institutions. Emphasis in this chapter is on the historical analysis as an aid to understanding the labor movement as a contemporary socioeconomic institution.

The U.S. labor movement has a uniquely American character. In order to appreciate this fact, one must know the history of these unions, or where they came from and why they developed in their own way. The authors make two attempts to aid the student in coping with the necessary brevity of the description. First, sources for more detailed reading are provided in the forms of footnotes and suggested readings. Second, a series of generalizations are introduced to provide a meaningful context in which to consider the selected historical accounts.

The labor movement[1] "enjoys" the questionable benefit that most Americans are convinced that they know a lot about it. Unfortunately, much of the presumed knowledge represents popular myth. The following set of generalizations may confirm this factor.

The U.S. labor movement is essentially a conservative institution. Most Americans view the labor movement as being somewhere between "liberal" and "radical." There is ample historical support for both the conservatism and the myth of radicalism. The myth of radicalism developed from the notion that union attempts to force employers to allow workers to organize and bargain collectively were attacks on capitalism, property rights, and employer prerogatives. The truth of the conservatism was born of early AFL recognition that its survival depended on its being as "American" as possible. Our national history is replete with examples of institutions which failed to "make it" simply because they were viewed as "un-American."

The American labor movement has been pragmatic throughout its history. With few exceptions, unions have defined progress exclusively in terms of wages, hours, and employment conditions. Part of this pragmatism derived from the conservatism. When institutions are conservative their conservatism precludes pursuit of certain broad issues. The labor movement distrusted and was reluctant to utilize government assistance until the depression of the 1930s. This reluctance promoted a preoccupation with issues like wages, hours, and employment conditions and the resulting pragmatism. In the final analysis, no one can bargain with employers about issues which are other than local and private in scope.

By contrast to these first two generalizations, the *U.S. labor history is marked by examples of substantial violence.* There are at least two very different evaluations of this violence. The traditional explanation contends that labor organizations, by their very nature, must first be able to take some power from management in order to enjoy any success. Conflict results because managements are reluctant to lose any of their traditional power. Presumably the greater the degree of reluctance to surrender power, the greater the degree of conflict and violence. This view holds that violence is increased by the historical willingness of public authorities to intervene on behalf of management.

The alternative view has been stated fully by Jeremy Brecher.[2] He contends that violence involving unions is but a small part of an overall "stream" of violence that began with the widespread strikes of the 1870s and continued almost uninterrupted to the student strikes and antiwar demonstrations of the late 1960s and early 1970s. This violence is a continuing effort by the people who are without social or economic power to seize from the establishment some reasonable degree of power. Those accepting this view interpret union violence not as an end in itself but as part of a larger and more significant effort. The historical materials below suggest that this view is exaggerated.

The fourth generalization is the simple observation that *unions have with few exceptions actively avoided any alliance with any nonlabor group.* The philosophy of this avoidance was a distrust which reciprocated the distrust of the labor movement by the rest of society.[3] Part of the labor movement's desire to "go it alone" was a function of past experience. This was true particularly of relations with almost all governments. Finally, much of labor's attitude toward involvement with nonlabor groups came from the desire of the AFL leadership to avoid sharing with persons outside the labor movement the credit for accomplishments. U.S. union leaders recognized that only positive accomplishments clearly attributable to the labor movement would attract and retain members.

Finally, *the U.S. labor movement has devoted its energies to organizing and assisting those workers who were easiest to organize.* During the first three-quarters of its existence, the AFL organized almost exclusively workers with identifiable and rather high skills. The first task of any institution is survival. Persons who attempt to criticize the labor movement for its lack of missionary spirit should recognize this need.

THE PERIOD OF NONUNIONISM

The earliest unions (usually composed of skilled craftsmen) date from the end of the eighteenth century and were concerned almost exclusively with local issues of wages, hours, and conditions of employment.[4] These unions devoted much attention to union security. One of the earliest court cases involving a union[5] concerned the issue of the "closed shop." The question in this case became whether a union could exist legally. Under British common law, on which much of our law was based, unions were generally considered illegal criminal conspiracies. The court held that the union was illegal and could not even exist because of its goals. The impact of this judicial position is discussed in Chapter 7. It is sufficient to note here that even at this very early date unionists were forced to recognize the potential adverse impact of court decisions.

Early unions were local in nature, admitted only workers with a specific skill, and were concerned only with issues directly affecting wages, hours, and employment conditions, Although the logic of these last two characteristics is apparent, some explanation is necessary regarding the characteristics of localism. The local orientation of early unions was examined definitively by John R. Commons almost a century ago.[6] He argued that the area of local union concern was determined by the dimensions of the market in which goods produced by its members were sold. If the products were sold in a national market, the union's orientation would be national; if sold in a local market, the orientation would be local. The nature of products produced by early union members (e.g., shoes, local transport, buildings, etc.) and the limited systems of early transportation explain the early unions' preoccupation with their local situations. The Commons description also explains some current union behavior, such as the local orientation of the building trades unions whose product is local, and the international orientation of unions like the United Automobile Workers.[7]

It was not until the decades of the 1820s and the 1830s that U.S. unions began to expand. This expansion was due largely to two factors: an improved transportation system and a need for political involvement. However, virtually all attempts at organization beyond the local area failed.

The early unions were unable to maintain organization during a general economic decline. For example, during the post-Napoleonic Wars' depression, most existing unions disappeared, in part because of decreased job opportunities and in part because many employers lowered wage rates, discharged workers, and/or did not honor earlier agreements for closed or union shops.[8]

The emerging labor movement also encountered difficulties with political action and intellectuals. It was concerned politically with reform issues—land reform, universal suffrage, free public education, etc. These issues involved direct participation in the political process, and the labor movement came into contact with persons who possessed substantial formal education but had little or no experience with manual labor. Most of these "intellectuals" saw the labor movement only as one part of a broad attempt to reform society. The labor movement reacted negatively and developed a distrust of intellectuals which continues widespread today among unions. Partially because of the infusion of this intellectual element and partially because of the labor movement's inexperience, these early attempts at political activity almost invariably failed.[9]

Labor movement activity was diverted to consumer and producer cooperatives in both the 1840s and, to a lesser extent, in the 1860s. This diversion occurred because U.S. workers were not "ready" for unions. Selig Perlman, the famous labor economist, observed nearly a half-century ago that, in order to have an interest in unions, workers must be convinced that they are and will be dependent on hourly wages for a living.[10] Workers were not convinced that they *really* were workers prior to the Civil War period. Instead they apparently felt that they were owners, managers, or entrepreneurs *in transit* and that cooperatives were a movement in that direction.

Despite these failures, the pre-Civil War period contained one positive event. An entirely new legal approach to unions emerged in 1842.[11] Common law criminal conspiracy doctrine was replaced by the concept of "means and ends." Instead of treating unions as illegal institutions per se, the courts evaluated both the union goals and means employed to achieve them in terms of existing public policy. If both the goals and the means employed were legal, then the union was legal. Although this change was very significant,[12] its impact on union growth and stability would not become apparent for at least several decades. The immediate pre-Civil War period was one of substantial union growth, particularly in the formation of new national or international unions.[13] However, the growth was short-lived, and virtually none of these unions survived the Civil War.

There were two significant occurrences in the immediate post-Civil War period. First, nearly all of the unions that had disbanded because of the war resumed operation. Second, there were several attempts (with varying degrees of success) to develop some type of national federation or interunion organization. The organizations were essentially reformist, very open in membership,[14] and moderately political. They were based on the notion of broad working class advance. These attempts at national organization carried the seeds from which the American Federation of Labor grew. A brief description of the Knights of Labor offers a general description of these various efforts.

Knights of Labor

The Noble Order of Knights of Labor was founded as a small local of the Philadelphia garment workers in 1869, and functioned as a secret organization for a decade. The organization grew slowly due to this secrecy. However, unprecedented success in a series of railroad strikes during the first half of the 1880s and the abandonment of secrecy caused the Knights' membership to expand from 10,000 (1879) to over 700,000 (1886). The Knights were a federation with a national assembly that exerted strong central control over state, district, and local bodies. The local assemblies were of two types. The "trade assemblies" were local craft unions; the "mixed assemblies" admitted workers from a wide range of occupations and professions. Although the Knights' general goal was replacement of a competitive economic society by a cooperative one, they had short-run goals also, including the eight-hour day, equal treatment for women, abolition of child and convict labor, public ownership of utilities, and establishment of both consumer and producer cooperatives. The Knights emphasized political and educational means rather than collective bargaining. Their leadership viewed the strike as a last and a poor alternative.

However, the period of the Knights' greatest success, the mid-1880s, was the period of their greatest resort to strikes[15] The reported membership of the Knights decreased from a record 700,000 in 1886 to only 100,000 in 1890. Reasons for their decline include inadequate national leadership, opposition from existing craft unions, and the loss of major strikes in meat packing and the railroads in 1886 and 1887.[16] The lasting significance of the Knights was the reassurance that reasonably well organized unions could mount successful strike efforts against powerful employers.[17]

THE PERIOD OF BUSINESS UNIONISM

The AFL

A new organization, the Federated Organization of Trades and Labor Union (FOTLU), was formed in 1881 because of dissatisfaction of many craft unions with the Knights. The founding unions indicated the direction of the organization. They included the printers, iron and steelworkers, molders, cigarmakers, carpenters, and glassworkers. The new organization was based on four principles: (1) complete autonomy of affiliated international unions in their internal affairs, (2) exclusive jurisdiction of affiliates with that jurisdiction respected by all affiliates,[18] (3) avoidance of any formal political attachment plus vigorous support of "friends" and opposition to "enemies," and (4) exclusive reliance on collective bargaining for the improvement of wages, hours, and working conditions. These principles proved so appealing that all existing national unions except the railroad brotherhoods affiliated within a short period. The FOTLU changed its name to the American Federation of Labor (AFL) in 1886.

The period immediately following the formation of the AFL included several significant developments. In the early 1890s, the first major U.S. industrial union, the United Mine Workers, was formed.[19] There were two of organized labor's most significant defeats also. In what proved to be a disastrous strike at Homestead, Pennsylvania, the Amalgamated Association of Iron, Steel, and Tin Workers (a founding member of the AFL) was eliminated from the steel industry for all practical purposes. It was not until almost half a century later, with the advent of the United Steelworkers, that the steel industry would have any significant union organization.[20] The second defeat involved the independent American Railway Union in the Pullman strike, which was a major reversal for the labor movement. Federal government intervention on behalf of management in this strike reinforced the AFL distrust of government. The failure of the American Railway Union, an industrial union, also ensured the future of exclusive craft unionism for future railroad workers.

It was perhaps prophetic that the major unions affilitated with the AFL survived the depression of the early 1890s, in membership and bargaining strength better than they had in any previous economic downturn. The post-depression period included one of the largest union membership increases ever (Table 1). Perhaps the most impressive result was the doubling of membership from 1897 to 1900 and again from 1900 to 1903.

TABLE 1

Total Membership of U.S. Unions, Selected Years, 1897-1906

Year	Membership	Year	Membership
1897	447,000	1902	1,375,900
1898	500,700	1903	1,913,900
1899	611,000	1904	2,072,700
1900	868,000	1905	2,022,300
1901	1,124,700	1906	1,958,700

Source: Leo Wolman, *The Growth of American Trade Unions: 1880-1923* (New York: National Bureau of Economic Research, 1924).

Industrial Workers of the World

The Industrial Workers of the World (IWW), the only significant challenge to the AFL prior to the depression of the 1930s, began near the end of the period depicted in Table 1, in 1905.[21] The IWW challenged the AFL philosophy by attempting to organize workers whom the AFL ignored— unskilled and semiskilled factory workers, lumberjacks, miners, and migrant workers—and seriously challenged the existing socioeconomic system. The following exerpt from the IWW constitution points to the latter difference:[22]

> The working class and the employing class have nothing in common . . .
>
> Between these two classes a struggle must go on until the workers of the world organize as a class, take possession of the earth and the machinery of production, and abolish the wage system . . .
>
> Instead of the conservative motto, 'a fair day's wage for a fair day's work,' we must inscribe on our banner the revolutionary watchword, 'abolition of the wage system.'
>
> It is the historic mission of the working class to do away with capitalism . . .

Although attendance at the IWW founding convention included elements ranging from traditional union leaders to avowed revolutionaries, the more conservative elements left the IWW within its first year or two. The remaining organization acquired a reputation as lawless and revolutionary. The IWW enjoyed marked success from 1910 to 1915, but the traditional U.S. reaction against organizations seeking major social changes began soon afterwards. This mounting public concern coupled with the IWW's internal dislike for organization produced its virtual disappearance by the middle of World War I. The contribution of the IWW was to remind the AFL and its leaders of some mistakes to be avoided and of the masses of workers not organized by the AFL.

Pre-World War I Period

The prewar period was generally a poor one for the labor movement. Union membership increased only from 2.1 million to 2.6 million persons from 1908 to 1915. More important, the period was one of adverse judicial decisions. First, federal courts began to subject unions directly to the Sherman Antitrust Act. The Supreme Court upheld a Sherman Act judgment of more than $500,000 against the Hatters Union in 1908.[23] The decision held that the union, by pursuing an economic strike and boycott, had interfered with the free flow of commerce. This decision meant that virtually all union economic activities were potential violations of the law. Any degree of success in economic activities would likely interfere with the flow of commerce.[24] As a result, the AFL engaged in its most significant legislative and political effort to that time.

However, what was thought to be a victory with passage of the Clayton Act proved a failure because of court interpretations.

World War I

During World War I, union membership increased significantly, particularly in industries involved in war production (Table 2). Much of organized labor's wartime success was due to President Woodrow Wilson's administration. The federal executive branch operated the railroads, made it clear to all government contractors that it favored unions and collective bargaining, appointed union leaders to important advisory positions, and was responsible for the labor-management conference of 1918 which produced the National War Labor Board (NWLB). The NWLB was significant because (1) it reduced strike activity that had developed from labor reaction to rising inflation of 1917, and (2) it represented the forerunner in form and spirit of much of the social and economic legislation of the 1930s.[25]

TABLE 2

Union Membership in Selected
Industries, 1916 and 1920 (thousands)

| | Membership | |
Industry	1916	1920
Transportation	623	1256
Seafaring	22	103
Longshoring	25	74
Teaming	59	110
Meat Packing	8	65

Source: Same as Table 1.

The 1920s

The postwar period was one of continued improvement for the labor movement. However, there were three negative events. The first was the Boston police strike. The strike itself had no great impact, but its implications were very important because they established this nation's general negative attitude toward organization, collective bargaining, and striking by public employees. Governor Calvin Coolidge called out the Massachusetts state militia and issued a statement that, "There is no right to strike against the public safety by anyone, anywhere, anytime."[26] The impact in terms of public employee unionism is discussed in Chapter 10.

The AFL enjoyed initial success in its one major postwar organizational drive, in the steel industry. The drive began with an AFL appeal for funds and organizing help from the 24 affiliated unions with jurisdictional interests in the steel industry. The theory was that once the industry was successfully organized each affiliated union would take those workers whose skills placed them in it. Little attention was given to the organizational disposition of the unskilled workers. Almost 100,000 workers were organized during the first 18 months. However, the AFL in mid-1919 made what proved a very costly tactical mistake by turning the drive directly to U.S. Steel. The company reacted by mounting what became virtually a "holy" crusade against the entire labor movement. Characterizing the organizing strike alternatively as a "plot hatched in Moscow" or "a war between revolutionaries and America,"[27] and making widespread use of strikebreakers, the company broke the effort against it and the rest of the industry. Labor had failed once again in basic steel.

The third event was internal. Samuel Gompers, AFL president since its inception except for one year, had grown old and tired. His passive leadership in the early 1920s coincided with a general counteroffensive by management. Following U.S. Steel's lead, many managements successfully characterized the labor movement as "red" or "soviet." Some advanced the idea of "The American Way" or "The American Plan." This assault consisted of either strong support for "company unions" or so-called "open shops." The latter were situations in which there was no union and were defended as protecting the individual worker's right to work. By the end of the decade, 1.5 million workers belonged to company unions compared to 3.5 million AFL members. The AFL membership in 1920 had been 5 million.

A power struggle developed when Gompers died in 1924. William Green, then vice-president of the United Mine Workers, was elected AFL president. He proved a weak, unfortunate choice, and the craft union presidents with little interest in membership expansion effectively operated the AFL until about the mid-point of the 1930s depression.

The U.S. fell victim to an economic downturn without precedent in 1929. By the end of the summer of 1932, the estimated unemployment was 25 percent of the civilian labor force. The labor movement suffered membership losses. For example, AFL membership decreased by approximately 33 percent, 1930-1935. Union membership as a percentage of the labor force was at its lowest point since 1890.

The Roosevelt Years

The years during which Franklin Roosevelt occupied the White House were remarkable ones for the U.S. economy. They were even more remarkable for the labor movement. It gained legal and institutional respectability during these years. The former was due largely to the Democratic Party administration; the latter was a tribute to the development and rise of the Congress of Industrial Organizations (CIO), known initially as the Committee for Industrial Organization.

The early and mid-1930s yielded a very rich legislative harvest for the labor movement. Beginning with the passage of the Norris-LaGuardia Act in 1932 and ending with the Social Security Act, minimum wage legislation, and the National Labor Relations (Wagner) Act, more progress was made in the legislative halls than in the entire past history of the labor movement. The labor movement, by abandoning its reluctance for political activity and by working vigorously with nonlabor reform groups, contributed significantly to this record. This departure by organized labor was particularly evident in the AFL's support of the minimum wage in the National Industrial Recovery Act and the Fair Labor Standards Act. The other force making this period a vital and innovative one was internal to the labor movement—the rise of industrial unionism.

THE PERIOD OF INDUSTRIAL UNIONISM

The CIO

The notion of industrial unionism was not new in 1935. The United Mine Workers had existed within the AFL almost from its inception. However, the problem generated by industrial unionism in the 1930s was quite different from the one that had existed previously. The traditional issue within the AFL had been whether to attempt organization of workers without a basic skill. When earlier attempts had failed, the AFL was spared a confrontation with the more important question of what to do with these workers once they were organized. However, literally thousands of workers had organized themselves into local industrial unions in the automobile, rubber, and steel industries by the mid-1930s. Many others were ready to organize in the cement, clothing, aluminum, and textile industries. The AFL response was traditional. Its Executive Council indicated a willingness to issue charters to these workers for "federal locals" which would be directly affiliated with the AFL and later be divided and integrated into appropriate existing craft unions. The AFL craft union presidents, who possessed the political power within the AFL, were either unwilling or unable to think in terms of industrial unions.

The AFL decision to create federal locals and to charter national unions in the automobile and rubber industries quieted the issue for a year.[28] However, many federal locals dropped their affiliation and others were absorbed illegally into traditional AFL craft unions looking for additional members during that year. This experience convinced some AFL leaders that the industrial union approach was essential. The issue became clearly drawn at the 1935 AFL convention when a resolution was introduced to stop all future organizing along industrial lines. After a long and bitter floor fight, the resolution passed. In November of 1935, the unions that had supported industrial organizing formed the Committee for Industrial Organization (CIO) with the avowed purpose of working within the AFL to promote industrial unionism. The group was rejected by the AFL Executive Council, charged with "dual unionism," and shortly thereafter dismissed from the AFL.[29]

The Wagner Act and World War II

Workers gained the legal right to organize and to bargain collectively with the passage of the Wagner Act in 1935. The Wagner Act and the CIO reacted on one another to produce the greatest organizational advance in the history of the U.S. labor movement. The increase in organized labor benefited both the AFL and the CIO. AFL membership increased from 2.1 million (1933) to 4.3 million (1940), and CIO membership reached 3.6 million during the same period. Although World War II was not as successful a period for the labor movement as World War I had been, it was one of significant growth and consolidation. For example, the early part of the period included the successful organization of the basic steel industry.

The performance of U.S. labor during the war was excellent.[30] This performance was due, in no small part, to the ability of the War Labor Board (WLB) to structure both acceptable and workable solutions to many problems. President Roosevelt created the WLB shortly after Pearl Harbor under his wartime emergency powers. The WLB's solution to the difficult issue of union security was development of the concept of "maintenance of membership." After some period of time, e.g., 30 days, a worker was required to decide whether to join a union. His decision remained in effect for one year with an annual opportunity to change his decision. One-third of all union members were working under such an agreement by the end of the war.[31]

The problem of wages and wartime inflation was resolved by the WLB's "Little Steel" formula which allowed wage increases to a maximum of 15 percent above the wage rate at the beginning of 1941. Higher increases required WLB approval. Union attempts to avoid this limitation through negotiation of increased fringe benefits led the WLB to extend the limitation to fringe benefit costs in 1943.

One impact of World War II was an expansion in employment of blacks in industry and a subsequent expansion in black membership in the CIO unions of the mass production industries. The CIO had a more open racial policy than the AFL, and its growth in black membership created greater stress between the AFL and CIO.

A second item of difference involved the presence of significant numbers of Communist Party members and sympathizers within CIO affiliates. The emerging CIO unions of the 1930s had accepted organizing assistance from all sources. With the coming of strained international relations in 1946, the role of communists in the CIO became a subject of public concern and an internal problem for the CIO. The issue of Communism among CIO affiliates virtually dominated postwar merger talks between the AFL and CIO. The CIO resolved the issue in 1948 by expelling several important affiliates with communist leadership.

The Postwar Period

The immediate postwar period was one of considerable labor unrest. Man-hours lost from strikes increased because almost every economist was convinced that the period would be one of high unemployment when, in fact, it was one of rapid inflation. Neither the public nor the President was in a mood to tolerate labor disputes. The results were passage of the Labor-Management Relations (Taft-Hartley) Act, and President Truman's taking every opportunity to intervene personally in major strikes. The public had become very disenchanted with the labor movement. The decisive action of the CIO in ridding itself of communism may have "saved" the labor movement in public opinion in 1948.

The Merger

Following CIO expulsion of its communist-dominated affiliates, the AFL and CIO began gradual work toward reunification. One move was their cooperation in the promotion of the Marshall Plan to assist the rebuilding of Europe. A second move was their cooperation in forming the United Labor Policy Committee during the Korean War. This cooperation and the public's unwillingness to tolerate jurisdictional disputes led to the AFL-CIO No-Raiding Pact of 1954.

By the early 1950s, nearly all of the major participants in the split of the 1930s had disappeared. Both William Green and Phillip Murray had died, and John L. Lewis had once again led his Mine Workers into an independent status. New leadership provided by George Meany (AFL) and Walter Reuther (CIO) seemed to be concerned with substantive rather than symbolic issues. The AFL had greatly increased the merger possibility by dealing finally with the issues of internal union corruption within some of its major affiliates. To this end, the AFL expelled the International Longshoremen's Union in 1953.[32]

In February of 1955, a formal merger agreement was concluded which gave the presidency of the combined organization to George Meany but which retained, in effect, the CIO intact as the Industrial Union Department of the new AFL-CIO. The Industrial Union Department organizational structure within the new federation protected the jurisdictional interests and rights of the old CIO unions. The new AFL-CIO went on record quickly in opposition to both racketeering and racial discrimination.

Recent Developments

As the decade of the 1960s evolved, many students of the labor movement perceived that something was wrong. One item cited frequently to support this perception was the static AFL-CIO membership which was 16 million in both 1955 and 1965. Although several factors combined to produce this stability, many observers contended it was evidence that the labor movement had lost its momentum. By the early 1950s, the "easy" part of the organizing task—the production and maintenance workers in northern manufacturing—had been completed. What remained were manufacturing workers in the South and white-collar workers. The latter were very difficult to organize because they saw themselves as either a part of management or as potential managers and thus failed to identify with labor organizations. Organizing efforts in the South outside of the largest urban areas encountered extremely hostile local receptions. There remained substantial numbers of unorganized workers in the trades and service industries. Management had become both much more sensitive and much more realistic in their attitudes and actions since the 1930s and 1940s.

By contrast, the mid-1960s saw the emergence of three counter-trends. First, there was a marked increase in organizing and bargaining by federal government employees under the Kennedy-Johnson administration. Second, other public employees showed increased interest in organizing. Finally, organizing among white-collar employees began to show positive results. The details of these trends are developed more fully in Chapters 6 and 10.

This concludes our survey of the evolution of the U.S. labor movement. We urge the student to review the five generalizations which began this chapter. In the final analysis, much of the activity of unions which is reported in the media can be understood by remembering these generalizations and some of the specifics in this chapter.

IMPORTANT NEW TERMS INTRODUCED

Craft union: A union whose membership is restricted to workers who possess an identifiable skill.

Industrial union: A union which allows into membership all workers in a given industry regardless of their skills (or lack of an identifiable skill).

Jurisdiction: The occupations, crafts, skills, industries, or geographic areas over which one union claims the exclusive right to organize workers.

SUGGESTED ADDITIONAL READINGS

Eli Chinoy, *Automobile Workers and the American Dream* (Garden City: Doubleday, 1955).

John R. Commons, et al., *History of Labor in the United States (New York:* Macmillan, 1935), Volumes I, II, and IV.

Melvyn Dubofsky (ed.), *American Labor Since the New Deal* (Chicago: Quadrangle Books, 1971).

Henry Pelling, *American Labor* (Chicago: University of Chicago Press, 1960).

Joseph G. Rayback, *A History of American Labor* (New York: Macmillan, 1966).

NOTES

[1] The term *labor movement* describes two different concepts throughout this book. One is the identifiable group of people who depend on unions. The other is the group of unions organized into a national body.

[2] Jeremey Brecher, *Strike* (San Francisco: Straight Arrow Books, 1972). Although the reader may disagree with Brecher's conclusions, the volume is an excellent demonstration of how to go about testing a historical thesis of this type.

[3] The reader seeking more detailed treatment of this subject is directed to Mollie Ray Cowell, *Labor and Politics: The Attitude of the American Federation of Labor Toward Legislation and Politics* (New York: Houghton Mifflin, 1925).

[4] An excellent analysis of the early unions' bargaining pursuits is found in Vernon H. Jensen, "Notes on the Beginning of Collective Bargaining," *Industrial and Labor Relations Review,* 9, No. 2 (January 1956). A detailed history of this period is John R. Commons and Associates, *History of Labor in the United States,* 2 Vols. (New York: Macmillan, 1918), a classic description.

[5] *Commonwealth v. Pullis.* It is most readily available in John R. Commons et al., *A Documentary History of American Industrial Society* (Cleveland: A. H. Clark, 1910), Vol. 50.

[6] See John R. Commons, "The American Shoemakers, 1648-1895," *Labor and Administration,* Chapter 14 (New York: Macmillan, 1913).

[7] See Karl F. Treakel, "World Auto Councils and Collective Bargaining," *Industrial Relations,* 11, No. 1 (February 1972), pp. 72-80, for a detailed analysis.

[8] Closed shop agreements require job seekers to be union members as a prerequisite to employment. Union shop agreements require membership after some period of time as a prerequisite to continued employment.

[9] Some students of this subject identify the capacity of established political parties in this country to assimilate any movement toward third parties as another cause for the failure. See William B. Hesseltine, *Third-Party Movements in the United States* (New York: Van Nostrand, 1966).

[10] See Selig Perlman, *A Theory of the Labor Movement* (New York: Augustus M. Kelley, 1949), pp. 237-253 for a complete discussion of this point.

[11] *Commonwealth v. Hunt,* Metcalf, Ill, Mass. 1842., reprinted in *Labor Law Course* (Chicago: Commerce Clearing House, 1967), pp. 216-220.

[12] The importance of this decision is discussed in greater detail in Chapter 7.

[13] The terms *national union* and *international union* are often used interchangeably. The distinction often means one union has locals in Mexico or Canada.

[14] Additional information on the first of these groups, the National Labor Union, is in Gerald N. Gros, "Reform Unionism; The National Labor Union," *Journal of Economic History* (Spring, 1954), pp. 126-142.

[15] See Gerald N. Gros, "The Knights of Labor, Politics, and Populism," *Mid-America,* 40, No. 1 (January 1958), pp. 3-21, and Gerald N. Gros, "The Knights of Labor and the Trade Unions, 1878-1886," *Journal of Economic History,* 28 (June 1958), pp. 176-192.

[16] Donald L, Kemmerer and Edward D. Wickersham, "Reasons for the Growth of the Knights of Labor in 1885-1886," *Industrial and Labor Relations Review,* 3, No. 2 (January 1950), pp. 213-220, is an excellent summary of the arguments.

[17] See Paul J. Carter, Jr., "Mark Twain and the American Labor Movement," *The New England Quarterly*, 30 (September 1957), pp. 382-388, for a somewhat unusual account of the Knights' activities.

[18] The term *jurisdiction* refers to those industries and occupations which a given union is chartered to organize.

[19] Craft unions organize only workers with the same identifiable skill, such as plumbers or carpenters. Industrial unions organize all workers regardless of skill who work in the same industry.

[20] R. I. Finch, "Unionism in the Iron and Steel Industry," *Political Science Quarterly*, 24 (1909), pp. 71-78, contains a detailed account of the Homestead strike. Almont Lindsay, *The Pullman Strike* (Chicago: University of Chicago Press, 1942) contains an excellent and rather detailed analysis of the Pullman strike as well as its noneconomic implications.

[21] Paul F. Brissenden, *The IWW: A Study of American Syndication* (New York: Columbia University Press, 1920) is the classic study of the IWW.

[22] *Songs of the Workers*, 29th ed. (Chicago: Industrial Workers of the World, 1956), p. 3.

[23] *Lawlor v. Loewe*, 235 U.S. 522, 35 Sup. Ct. 170.

[24] The entire question of antitrust coverage of labor organizations is treated in greater detail in other chapters. Detailed analysis of organized labor's involvement in these issues is found in Stanley I. Kutler, "Labor, the Clayton Act, and the Supreme Court," *Labor History*, 3, No. 1 (Winter, 1962), pp. 18-30; and in A. T. Mason, *Organized Labor and Law, with Especial Reference to the Sherman and Clayton Acts* (Durham: Duke University Press, 1925).

[25] For example, see Foster R. Dulles, *Labor in America* (New York: Thomas Y. Crowell, 1949), pp. 226-228.

[26] See William Allen White, *a Puritan in Babylon: The Story of Calvin Coolidge* (New York: Macmillan, 1938), p. 166.

[27] The company took full advantage of the postwar "red" reaction which is described in Robert K. Munay, *Red Scare: A Study in National Hysteria, 1919-1920* (New York: McGraw-Hill, 1964).

[28] Although industrial unions were chartered in both industries, President Green appointed an old-line AFL craft unionist as president of the new union.

[29] "Dual unionism" describes establishment of a new union whose jurisdiction duplicates that of an existing union or joining of such a new union, and is one of the few really "dirty words" of the labor movement.

[30] The best single work on labor during World War II is Joel Seidman, *American Labor from Defense to Reconversion* (Chicago: University of Chicago Press, 1953).

[31] Henry Pelling, *American Labor* (Chicago: University of Chicago Press, 1961), pp. 176-178.

[32] A more detailed academic account of the racketeering issues is contained in Philip Taft, *Corruption and Racketeering in the Labor Movement* (Ithaca: New York State School of Industrial and Labor Relations, 1958).

6

The Unions Today

Organized labor or the unions and their officials are very much in the news and before the public. Because of the media coverage, more citizens probably know the name of the president of the American Federation of Labor-Congress of Industrial Organizations (AFL-CIO) than know the names of some of their elected governmental officials. And they probably know in a general way that organized labor is seeking increased wages or better fringe benefits or is supporting or opposing this government policy or that one. Yet most citizens, including some businessmen and governmental officials, understand little about the actual structure of organized labor (Figure 1), its goals and the ways in which they are formulated, and the functions of its various components. Therefore, this chapter contains an outline of the structure and government of organized labor, its present and future goals, and the characteristics that make it unique among labor movements in the world.

STRUCTURE AND GOVERNMENT

The Local Union

The nearly 80,000 local unions in this country are the basis on which the entire labor movement is built. They are the units of union government with which the rank-and-file union member can identify. Their officers are his

63

FIGURE 1   *The Structure of Organized Labor*

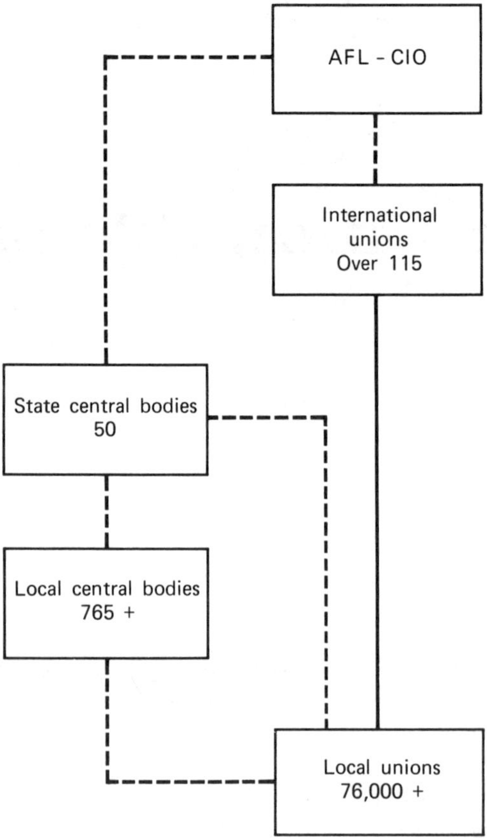

coworkers and former coworkers; the contract which these officers negotiate and administer is his contract. These officers are also the ones who attempt to solve any problems in working conditions that he may encounter. Thus, the success or failure of organized labor in attracting the support of its membership depends ultimately upon the efficiency with which the local union functions.

The local union and its officers perform several basic tasks. First, they negotiate all or a portion of the collective bargaining agreement (see Chapter 9) which determines the wages, hours, and working conditions of the employees. Second, they must administer this agreement, making certain that the employer fulfills his responsibilities to the union and the employees. This task is undertaken most frequently through the mechanism of the "grievance procedure," which provides an orderly process through which employee complaints are considered (see Chapter 10). Third, the officers and members of the local union attempt to "organize" (persuade nonmembers to join the union) all of the employees at their place of work or at other establishments which may not be covered by a collective bargaining agreement (i.e., nonunion establishments). Finally, the officers attempt to implement the policies of their international union with respect to contract terms, employment practices, etc. These activities are financed by the payment of monthly dues to the local union by its members.

The number of officers in a local union, their titles, and their responsibilities vary greatly in accordance with the industry, the international union, the number of members, and various other factors. However, we can outline some of the more common offices of a local union. In all instances, officers are elected by the membership, in accordance with their constitution and by-laws, at a regular (usually monthly) or special membership meeting; the regular meeting is the supreme governing body of the local union. Officers serve for a specified term, not to exceed three years, and may be and often are reelected.

The president of the local union presides at the membership meetings and provides leadership to the members. The secretary-treasurer[1] maintains the local union's financial and other records. These two offices may be full-time salaried positions in a large local union but are more likely to be part-time with only a nominal salary and to be occupied by persons who continue to work at their regular employment. If the local union is sufficiently large and solvent, there may be a business agent also. He performs the daily administrative tasks, supervises expenditures and any staff, provides organizing leadership, plays a prominent role in negotiations, and offers various types of assistance to the president and secretary-treasurer.[2] He is full-time and salaried.

The shop stewards or committeemen, who may be elected or appointed, occupy a critical position in the official structure of the local union. There will be one steward for each department or division or for some specified number of employees. The steward is allowed a specified amount of time each week to conduct union business during his normal working hours. Such business consists normally of processing grievances under the labor-management agreement. Therefore, he must possess a good knowledge of the terms of the agreement and must have a thorough understanding of the nature of the work in his department. He is the individual with whom the union is most likely to be identified by the rank-and-file member.[3] Stewards seldom receive compensation for their work. However, they may have "superseniority" which means that they would be the last persons to be laid off; and some international unions provide training for them.

The International Union

The importance of the international union[4] has been increasing because of the large number of national contracts and the emergence of both national markets in many industries and the conglomerate form of enterprise. The international union governs its affiliated local unions in a general way and offers them services. The local union receives a charter when it affiliates with the international union. In extreme cases, the international union might revoke this charter. In most instances of problems with the local union (e.g., financial malpractice, corruption, mismanagement, failure to meet obligations, etc.), the international union invokes a "trusteeship" arrangement in accordance with its constitution if the problem is sufficiently severe. Under such an arrangement, the local officers are removed, the funds attached, and a "trustee" appointed to manage the local union until the problem can be corrected.

Most international unions provide assistance to their local unions in negotiations and offer strike benefits to striking members. Often there are various service departments of the international union, staffed by professionals, which aid the local unions. A research department provides statistics to assist with the union's bargaining position. A legal department helps with the writing of agreements and with the conduct of National Labor Relations Board proceedings. An education department provides training for local officers. These are but three examples of many types of service departments present in international unions. The international union also employs field representatives to assist with specific local problems.

The operations of the international union are financed through the payment of "per-capita" dues by the local union. Each local union is required to pay to the international union each month an amount per member fixed by the international union constitution. The governing body of the international union is its convention to which each local union sends delegates elected by its members. Each local union is usually accorded a certain number of votes based on the size of its membership. At the convention, the delegates elect the international officers, receive reports from these officers, make any necessary changes in the international union constitution, and conduct any other necessary business. Between conventions, the union's business is conducted by an executive board (i.e., a board of directors) composed of the international union officers.

Like the local union, the number and titles of officers of the international unions vary. Most often there is a president who conducts the union business between executive board meetings, appoints the staff of the international union, and chairs the convention. The secretary-treasurer maintains the records of the international union, supervises its finances and investments, and collects the per-capita dues from the local unions. Several vice-presidents may be elected either on a national or regional basis. Sometimes they have specific responsibilities, such as administration of a geographic region; in other unions, they may not.[5]

The AFL-CIO

The AFL-CIO is by far the most prominent element in the structure of organized labor. Yet, although it is a very significant element, it is more a "creature" of its affiliated international unions than a body which exists in hierarchical relationship. Although the AFL-CIO has the power to revoke the charter of, suspend, or expel an affiliate, it exists primarily to serve its affiliates. These services are provided in various ways. The Trade and Industrial Departments, each with a professional staff, work to promote the common interests of groups of affiliates (i.e., Building Trades, Industrial Union, Label Trades, Maritime Employees, Metal Trades, and Railway Employees) in legislative action, research, etc. Various operating departments with professional staff (i.e., Civil Rights, Community Services, Education, International Affairs, etc.) provide research, educational, and legislative services and assist the officers of the AFL-CIO. The AFL-CIO's voluntarily-financed Committee on Political Education works with the affiliated international and local unions in political campaigns to support candidates favorable to organized labor and its goals.[6] The work of the AFL-CIO is financed through the payment of per-capita dues to it by affiliated international unions.

The governing body of the AFL-CIO is its convention held every two years to which the affiliated international unions send elected delegates in accordance with their membership (Figure 2). The delegates elect officers, consider the reports of officers and committees, adopt resolutions, and may alter the constitution. An executive council composed of the president, secretary-treasurer, and 27 vice-presidents governs between conventions. The president is responsible for the general administration of the AFL-CIO, the appointment of staff, and service as the official national spokesman of the AFL-CIO. The secretary-treasurer maintains the records of the AFL-CIO and is responsible for the management of its finances. A general board composed of the members of the executive council, the principal officer of each affiliated international union, and the principal officer of each affiliated department, meets at least once each year to consider issues brought to it by the executive council.

State and Local Central Bodies

There are local central bodies in some 800 communities which are called variously City Central Labor Council, City AFL-CIO, etc. They serve to unite the local unions in the community which are AFL-CIO affiliates for cooperative actions in labor-management disputes, political campaigns, and community problems. Their work is financed by per-capita dues or affiliation fees from affiliated local unions. The president of the city central body may or may not be a fulltime salaried official depending upon the size and work of the central body. He serves as the official spokesman for organized labor in the community and gives administrative leadership. If the central body is sufficiently large, there may be a secretary-treasurer and other officers.

The state central bodies unite affiliated local unions and city central bodies on a statewide basis for cooperative action and legislative and political activities. They are usually located in the state capitol. There are usually a

FIGURE 2   *AFL-CIO Structure*

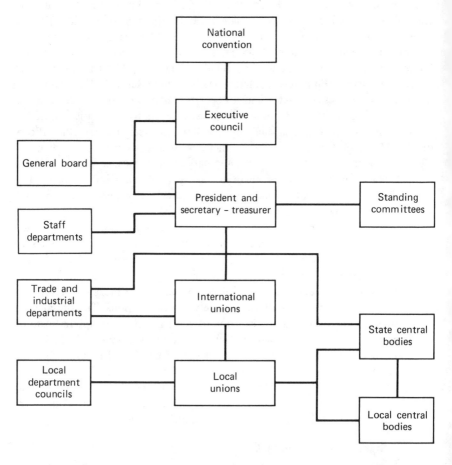

full-time president and secretary-treasurer plus some vice-presidents, all of whom are elected at the convention of the state central body to which affiliates send delegates. There may be professional staff to assist these officers.

UNION MEMBERSHIP

Although union membership is approximately 19 million persons, it has decreased to about 28 percent of the nonagricultural labor force from over 30 percent in the 1950s (Table 1). The percentages of the labor force organized vary greatly among industries, occupations, and regions. The membership tends to be concentrated among the largest international unions. Over 50 percent of total union membership in the United States is included in just five industrial groups (Table 2). The states of California, New York, and Pennsylvania include

TABLE 1

Union Membership as a Percentage
of the Nonagricultural Labor Force
for Selected Years, 1930 to 1968

Year	Percentage of nonagricultural labor force
1930	11.6
1935	13.2
1940	26.9
1945	35.5
1950	31.5
1955	33.2
1960	31.4
1965	28.4
1968	28.4

Source: U.S. Department of Labor, *Handbook of Labor Statistics, 1968*

TABLE 2

Distribution of Union Membership
Among Selected Industries, 1968

Industry	Percentage of total members
Metals, machinery, and	14.8
equipment	14.8
Transportation and	
public utilities	13.6 (*est.*)
Contract construction	13.0
Transportation equipment	6.7
Clothing, textiles, and	
leather	6.8
Federal government	5.0
Food, beverages, and	
tobacco	5.9
Services	6.5
Furniture, lumber, wood,	
and paper	4.5
State and local government	3.1
Printing and publishing	2.0
Mining and quarrying	1.8
Stone, clay, and glass	1.4
Agriculture	(less than 1.0)
Finance, insurance	(less than 1.0)

Sources: *Statistical Abstract, 1970* and *Manpower Report of the President, 1970*

over 33 percent of total union membership, while 21 states have uion membership that constitutes less than 25 percent of the labor force.[7] Union membership is much higher among semiskilled and skilled "blue-collar" workers than among "white-collar" workers. These facts have produced dire predictions by some persons about the future of orgainzed labor in the United States.

Yet these predictions have not proved correct to date, and organized labor continues to exercise a significant influence in the social and economic life of the nation. In part, this success by unions is due to the passage of legislation permitting government employees, including teachers, to organize for collective bargaining in many states. The unions of government employees are among the most rapidly growing.[8] By contrast, success in efforts to organize other types of "white-collar" workers has been limited.

Union efforts to organize workers in the South, an area in which employment is expanding, have met with some success, but the percentages of workers organized remain small compared to those in the rest of the nation. For example, less than one worker in ten is a union member in North Carolina and South Carolina. Therefore, organized labor must maintain and accelerate its organizing success among workers in the expanding industries and geographic areas if it is to continue as a significant factor in the economic and social life of the nation.

An additional factor which will affect the success of organized labor is the attitude toward it and toward its goals expressed by the general public and, even more significantly, by its members. A 1967 Harris poll indicated that 62 percent of the persons interviewed felt that union leaders' encouragement of strikes was a major cause of strikes. A 1965 Roper poll indicated that only 7 percent of the persons interviewed felt that union leaders were doing the most good for the country compared with percentages of 12 for business leaders, 26 for religious leaders, 31 for government leaders, and 12 for the Congress. In the same series of polls, the largest percentage of persons responded that union leaders were doing the least good for the country and that they believed least the speeches by labor leaders.[9] Thus, a large percentage of the general public regard union leaders and their goals with, at best, suspicion and perhaps hostility. Such a finding emphasizes the problems inherent in attempts to increase union membership and in attempts to obtain legislation favorable to the interests of organized labor.

ORGANIZING GOALS

In response to a question from the editor of a national magazine, the president of the United Automobile Workers Union stated that:[10]

> The groups of workers we traditionally have represented are growing smaller. There has been a union breakthrough among white-collar

employees, but mainly in government. As for office workers in the auto industry, managements give them the same raises the union wins for production workers, and frequently add something extra for the office group.

Similarly the president of the Communications Workers of America has observed that:[11]

> The young worker never experienced the big Depression. He is well educated, and has been taught to be independent. He doesn't feel the work ethic that is so important to his parents. Young workers don't have a clear idea of what they want, any more than young people ever did. So the labor movement must be flexible and keep up with change. A lot of us aren't flexible enough. That's why organized labor is not keeping up with the growth of the labor force.

These statements illuminate both some of the primary organizational goals and the failures to achieve those goals. In a labor force that is growing younger on the average and that is increasingly employed in white-collar occupations and in nonproduction industries, the percentage of union organization is decreasing (Figure 3). As the previous section on membership indicated, the newer industrial groups, the South, and also the younger workers pose the major prospects as well as the major problems for union organization.

The Young Worker

Several years ago, the AFL-CIO Department of Organization commissioned a study of the attitudes of voters in National Labor Relations Board elections in California.[12] The results of the study provide certain voter profiles:[13]

> The pro-union voter in a National Labor Relations Board election is most likely to be a stable, well-informed person who has invested several years on the job he holds when the election is held.

> There is a better than average chance that the sympathetic voter is married and a woman, and a good chance this voter is under 25.

> Conversely, the anti-union voter is indecisive, conservative and often motivated by confusion as to what union representation will do for him. . . .

> One [myth] which the survey burst involves the current belief that young people are generally alienated from much of society, including the trade union movement. Young people voted for the union at a rate within 4 percent of the overall pro-union average . . . more of those working on a job less than one year reported voting for the union than against.

FIGURE 3 *Growth in Union Membership*

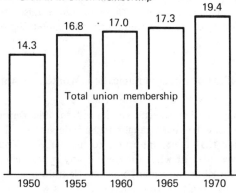

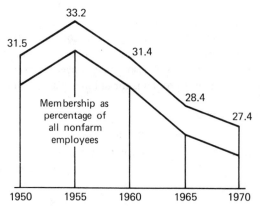

Source: Reprinted from *U. S. News and World Report,*
February 21, 1972. Copyright U. S. News and World
Report, Inc.

Interviewers in this survey discovered the following ranking of reasons why persons voted in favor of a union:[14]

1. Union representation and collective bargaining ensure better pay and job security.
2. Improved fringe benefits such as pensions, holidays and sick leave.
3. Fair pay, fairness in promotions, seniority rights.
4. Grievance procedure. (Older workers tended to rank this higher.)
5. Better control over speedup, production standards and quotas.

Therefore, this study indicates that union organization may not be as badly hindered by the increasing proportion of young people in the labor force as thought previously. Women may prove to be a source of increased union membership also.

White-Collar and Nonproduction Workers

The overall picture of union organization among white-collar workers is not promising at present. In 1968 and 1969, organization of white-collar workers actually decreased. In part, this result has come from the disinterest of many production worker union members in the organization of their white-collar counterparts. In part, it is due to the lack of knowledge by many unions on the proper approach to organizing such workers. The major factor may be one that has been mentioned by the United Automobile Workers Union president:[15]

> Office workers have told us frankly that they are content to stay out of the union because they don't have to pay dues or go on strike but get the same raises. They admit it's the union that wins them their raises.

There is some indication that the economic slump of 1971-75 may be a factor that will have a positive influence on union organization among many white-collar and technical employees who, for the first time, are finding themselves threatened with unemployment and are seeking methods of job security.

However, although the extent of white-collar organization remains limited, the organization of government employees at all levels of government has increased rapidly. The State, County, and Municipal Employees Union increased its membership by 150 percent during the decade of the 1960s, and the Retail Clerks International Union in the private sector nearly doubled its membership during the same period. The American Federation of Teachers has grown to some 250,000 members, and the National Education Association, which is increasingly functioning like a union, has over 1 million members. Over 1 million federal employees are union members.

DISTINCTIVE CHARACTERISTICS

The U.S. labor movement has undergone a long, often painful, evolution to its present state. It remains unique in many ways among the labor movements of the world and fails to conform to general characteristics in many other ways. Some of the characteristics which set the U.S. unions apart from other world unions are listed below.

Structure and government. In many nations, there are one or more "federations" which exercise virtual control over the policies of organized labor, supporting general strikes of all organized workers, engaging in national political activity, and acting as the major repository of union finances. Wage policies are established at a national level. In addition, there are so-called "general" unions that include among their memberships workers in virtually any occupation or industry. In contrast, there are over 100 U.S. national unions, each organized on an industrial or occupational (or multiindustrial or multioccupational) basis and affiliated in most cases with a national federation for whom they provide the financial support. Each remains independent in its wage policies and other matters.

Political activity. The union organizations of most Western nations are allied with political or sociopolitical groups. In many instances, the groups with whom they are aligned espouse an economic doctrine (i.e., Communist Party, democratic socialists) or have a religious basis. This alignment means that the policies of the unions may reflect political as well as economic goals and may be designed to foster the aims of a particular political group. Often this involves the existence of a "labor" party, which may be seeking industrial nationalization or worker control, through the government, of industry. Since the inception of the American Federation of Labor, U.S. unions have been active in the support of political *candidates* favorable to their aims. This support has not included alliance on a continuing basis with one political party or the development of a labor party.

Bargaining issues. Until recently, U.S. unions have restricted their priorities in collective bargaining to issues related directly to the well-being of the worker in his role as an employee, i.e., wages, hours, conditions of work, job security, retirement, etc. Decisions on the executive management of the firm (type of product produced, marketing, corporate structure, etc.) have been left to the employer. Because of the two previously mentioned factors, bargaining in other nations has included issues that are far broader in scope and include more basic decisions on the executive management of the firm.

IMPORTANT NEW TERMS INTRODUCED

Central body: An AFL-CIO organization in a city or state that unites and coordinates AFL-CIO affiliated local unions and their activities.

Trusteeship: A procedure through which local union officers are removed, the local union funds attached, and one or more persons appointed to administer the local union's affairs.

SUGGESTED ADDITIONAL READINGS

Marten Estey, *The Unions: Structure, Development, and Management* (New York: Harcourt, Brace, and World, 1967), 125 pp., provides an excellent summary of the way in which unions are structured and function.

J. Joseph Loewenberg and Michael H. Moskow (eds.), *Collective Bargaining in Government: Readings and Cases,* (Englewood Cliffs, N.J.: Prentice-Hall, 1971), 362 pp., brings together a series of articles on most of the major aspects of collective bargaining among public employees.

Leonard R. Sayles and George Strauss, *The Local Union,* rev. ed. (New York: Harcourt, Brace, and World, 1967), 174 pp., contains an "inside" picture of the operations and the problems of a local union.

NOTES

[1] Some local unions have a secretary and a treasurer or a recording secretary and a financial secretary. For simplicity, we have described the most common arrangement of a secretary-treasurer here.

[2] In some unions, such as those in the clothing industry, the business agent is the key officer of the local union. In these cases, the office will exist regardless of the size of the local union, with the international financing the office if necessary.

[3] An excellent description of the workings of a local union is provided in Leonard R. Sayles and George Strauss, *The Local Union,* rev. ed. (New York: Harcourt, Brace, and World, 1967), 174 pp.

[4] Most national unions have local unions in Canada and are thus called "international."

[5] The interrelationships among the elements of organized labor are detailed in Martin Estey, *The Unions: Structure, Development, and Management* (New York: Harcourt, Brace and World, 1967), 125 pp.

[6] Provisions of the Labor-Management Relations Act (1947) prohibit the use of union funds for the support of a candidate for federal office. C.O.P.E. and similar groups solicit funds from union members on a voluntary basis to provide such support and to finance voter registration campaigns and publicity.

[7] See U.S. Department of Commerce, *Statistical Abstract, 1974* (Washington: U.S. Government Printing Office, 1974) for a variety of statistics on union membership.

[8] See Daniel H. Kruger and Charles T. Schmidt, Jr. (eds.), *Collective Bargaining in the Public Service* (New York: Random House, 1969) for a series of studies that offer insight into the organizing of public employees.

[9] Summaries of these polls and an excellent analysis of their significance are contained in Derek C. Bok and John T. Dunlop, *Labor and the American Community* (New York: Simon and Schuster, 1970), pp. 12-30.

[10] "Is Labor Movement Losing Ground?" a copyrighted article in *U.S. News and World Report,* February 21 1972, p. 23.

[11] Ibid., p.25.

[12] See William L. Kircher, "Yardstick for More Effective Organizing," *The American Federationist* (March 1969), pp. 21-23.

[13] Ibid., p. 23.

[14] Ibid., p. 23.

[15] "Is Labor Movement Losing Ground?" p. 23.

7

The Evolution of
Labor Law
in the United States

The status and content of collective bargaining, the powers and limitations of the parties to bargaining, and the role of organized labor in both the economy and society have changed extensively during the nearly 200-year history of the United States. Unions have been transformed from weak, often secret, organizations subject to criminal prosecution for their bargaining activities into often powerful organizations that affect every aspect of our economic life. The open hostility of employers whose "industrial relations" budgets were composed of ammunition expenditures has changed to a toleration of a necessary "evil" with consequent expenditures for "human relations" activities and for the manipulation of opinion. Each of these changes was influenced significantly by alterations in the scope and substance of the law of collective bargaining which has grown from legislation and court decisions. We shall trace some of the highlights of this evolution of labor law in what follows.

FROM CONSPIRACY TO INJUNCTION: THE NINETEENTH CENTURY

Colonial Period

Unions developed slowly in America for several reasons. The employees or journeymen, as they were known, worked closely with their employers, known as masters, in small shops. The earnest and thrifty journeyman could save his wages and eventually become a master and, thus, did not see himself as a member of a "working class." Free workers were a minority in the labor force because slaves and indentured servants constituted the majority. Finally, and perhaps most importantly, a constant labor shortage kept American wages above those of Europe. These high wages prompted one of the first pieces of American labor legislation. The colonial authorities in New England enacted legislation that set maximum wages, prohibited occupational changes, and prescribed various modes of dress according to one's class.[1] The Massachusetts General Court established wage ceilings for several skilled occupations in 1630. However, the labor shortage rather than the legislation ruled employers' wage decisions in practice.

The Revolutionary War diminished the labor supply still further and increased the wage level, although some serious inflation accompanied it. This inflation encouraged some groups of workers to protest their wages and working conditions. However, these groups were not what we would call "unions" in the present sense of the term. The advent of unions awaited the end of the Revolutionary War and the postwar period when various changes in the economy and in industrial organization occurred.

Post-Revolutionary War Era

Several factors influenced the development of unions during the closing years of the eighteenth century. Producers were beginning to market their goods in a wider area and competition was increasing. One of the ways in which they sought to meet competition was the diminution of wages and/or the lengthening of the working hours. These efforts were facilitated by the increased scale of industry and the introduction of new production techniques that made possible the employment of less skilled workers, such as women, children, and immigrants. The first unions began to organize in an effort to meet these challenges to their status. They were small, craft unions composed exclusively of skilled workers.

The first union that had any permanency was the Federal Society of Cordwainers formed in Philadelphia in 1794.[2] Many of these early "journeymen societies" became quite militant and engaged in strikes and boycotts to support their positions, sometimes successfully. When economic weapons proved insufficient to meet the new unions, employers turned to the courts with increasing frequency.

The Conspiracy Doctrine

The attitude of the courts is reflected in an 1806 decision involving the Cordwainers of Philadelphia. They had struck their employers in an effort to obtain wage increases. In an indictment against them, they were charged with:[3]

... [combining and conspiring] to prevent by threats, menaces, and other unlawful means, other artificers, workmen, and journeymen in the said art and occupation [from working] . . .

The union members who were defendants were charged by the prosecutor with, "undertaking by a combination, to regulate the price of labour of others as well as their own."[4] The judge ruled that the defendants were guilty because:[5]

A combination of workmen to raise their wages may be considered in a two-fold point of view; one is to benefit themselves . . . the other is to injure those who do not join their society. The rule of law condemns both . . .

This decision, and similar ones, ushered in what has come to be called the "conspiracy doctrine" in labor relations. It derived from the common law principle that when two or more persons conspired to do something together (in this case, refuse to work), even though each could do it alone legally, they were guilty of a conspiracy against the public interest.

The conspiracy doctrine received a severe, if not fatal, reversal in the case of *Commonwealth v. Hunt* in 1842. Seven members of the Boston Journeymen Bootmakers Society were indicted and convicted for organizing a strike against an employer who hired a worker who was not a member of their union. In effect, they were seeking a closed shop.[6] Their conviction was reversed by the Massachusetts Supreme Court in a decision written by Chief Justice Shaw.[7] He ruled that the aim of the strike was to get all workers in the craft to join the union in order to increase its bargaining power, and that there was nothing illegal about wanting to achieve these objectives. He went on to state that the purposes of a union were lawful. In other words, the power that the union sought was to be used for a legal purpose, and, thus, the seeking of the power was legal.

Unions and the Injunction

During the nineteenth century, the employees of the Pullman Company shops which engaged in the manufacture of sleeping cars were required to live in a "model" company town. With the advent of the 1893 depression, the company dismissed over one-half of its shop employees and reduced the wages of the remainder by up to 40 percent, without offering any reductions in the rent that the employees were compelled to pay for their houses in the company town and without any reduction in the dividends paid to the firm's stockholders.[8] A committee of workers met with company officials to present their grievances and were dismissed the next day. This action precipitated a series of "escalations" in the controversy. The employees of the Pullman Company were organized extensively by the independent American Railway Union (ARU) and struck the company; the company responded by closing its plants.

The ARU had many operating employees of the various railroads among its membership. After the firings of the committee and the calling of the strike, the company refused to arbitrate the grievances. In response, the ARU operating employees refused to handle any train that included a Pullman car. The railroads, in turn, announced that they would fire any employee doing so. When the ARU declared that an entire crew would quit if any member of it were so fired the result was a virtual halt to rail service.

The railroad managers imported strikebreakers from Canada with instructions to couple U.S. Mail cars to any train with a Pullman car, and persuaded the Attorney General to swear in railroad security personnel as special deputies. When violence occurred between the strikebreakers, special deputies, and strikers, the railroad managers requested successfully that President Cleveland send federal troops "to protect the mails." Then they obtained a federal court injunction[9] against interference with the mails. The ARU President, Eugene Debs, offered to end the strike if the strikers were rehired without discrimination. After this request was denied and the strike continued, Debs and other union leaders were arrested, convicted of violation of an injunction, and the strike lost. The message of the Pullman strike was clear to unions and employers alike; the injunction had become an important weapon in the arsenal of those seeking to handicap unions. For more than 30 years, employers would be able to secure injunctions against what would be considered legitimate union activities today.

THE ISSUE OF UNIONS AS MONOPOLIES

The question of whether unions should be considered monopolies has provoked debate for many years.[10] The basic issue is whether unions can be considered "sellers" of labor in the economic sense. If so, then they could be considered monopolists on the grounds that they determine wages and working conditions for all workers in an organized unit. The alternative viewpoint is that labor is not a commodity and, thus, that no one is regarded reasonably as a seller of it other than the individual. These issues received considerable attention from the courts during the early part of this century because of the passage of two legislative acts.

The Sherman Act

Many large industrial complexes were formed during the latter years of the nineteenth century through mergers and the absorption of smaller firms by larger ones. The so-called "robber barons" who formed some of these complexes eliminated virtually all competition in certain product markets either through acquisition of control over all of the producers or by negotiation of collusive agreements on price and/or output with the remaining competitors. Popular concern that they might exploit this market control to the detriment of the consuming public and small firms prompted passage of the Sherman Anti-trust Act of 1890.[11] Section 1 of the Sherman Act provided that:

> ... every contract, combination in the form of trust or otherwise, or conspiracy, in restraint of trade or commerce among the several States or with foreign nations, is hereby declared to be illegal ... Every person who shall make any contract or engage in any combination or conspiracy hereby declared to be illegal shall be deemed guilty of a misdemeanor, and on conviction thereof shall be punished by fine not exceeding fifty thousand dollars, or by imprisonment not exceeding one year, or by both ...

and Section 2, that:

> Every person who shall monopolize, or attempt to monopolize, or combine or conspire with any other person or persons, to monopolize any part of the trade or commerce among the several States, or with foreign nations shall be deemed guilty of a misdemeanor ...

The Attorney General was empowered to initiate criminal prosecutions, and jurisdiction was given to the federal courts. However, anyone injured by violation of the law was allowed to bring civil suit for triple damages against the violator of the law in addition to the criminal penalties. This legislation exceeded the common law prohibition against restraint of trade in which courts refused simply to enforce agreements to restrain trade.

Restraint of trade implied the control of the supply or price of a commodity through denial or suppression of free enterprise under common law. This interpretation meant necessarily that a violator would have to be someone who produced or marketed a commodity. Therefore, the question of whether unions were covered by the Sherman Act was unclear, and the lower federal courts were split on this matter during the first 18 years of the Sherman Act. However, the question reached the U.S. Supreme Court in 1908 in the case of *Loewe v. Lawlor* or the "Danbury Hatters'" case.[12] A national union of hatters had organized most large manufacturers of felt hats, but the remaining unorganized firms offered severe price competition to the organized firms on the basis of the payment of lower wages. In an effort to organize Loewe's, one of the remaining nonunion firms, the union, and the American Federation of Labor (AFL) organized a national secondary boycott of retailers selling Loewe's hats.[13] AFL members were asked not to purchase Loewe's hats or to patronize retailers who sold them. The successful boycott led to cancellation of orders for Loewe's hats and subsequent losses by the firm.

Utilizing the Sherman Act, Loewe brought suit successfully for triple damages against the members of the hatters' union and was awarded over half a million dollars. The Supreme Court upheld the decision in favor of Loewe. The decision rested on Loewe's showing that the union's actions had interfered with the interstate shipment of its hats and with the intrastate fulfillment of his orders, although the Act did not mention "interference" and no evidence was present that the boycott was an attempt to control supply or price. Several aspects of this decision concerned union leaders. First, it outlawed effectively the secondary boycott. Second, it seemed to limit seriously the use of interstate strikes. Finally, a precedent seemed to be established of holding individual union members, rather than the union as an entity, liable for damages.

As a result of these concerns, union leaders worked successfully for passage of the Clayton Act, which amended the Sherman Act in a way designed to remove unions from its coverage. So enthusiastic was AFL President Samuel Gompers that he called the new legislation "Labor's Magna Charta."[14] He had reason for this strong statement of optimism. Section 6 of the Clayton Act declared that:[15]

> ... the labor of a human being is not a commodity or article of commerce. Nothing contained in the antitrust laws shall be construed to forbid the existence and operation of labor ... organizations instituted for the purposes of mutual help, and not having capital stock or conducted for profit ... from lawfully carrying out the objects thereof ... nor shall such organizations or the members thereof, be held or construed to be illegal combinations or conspiracies in restraint of trade, under the antitrust laws.

The section expressed the congressional intent to remove unions from prosecution as conspiracies under the antitrust laws. Section 20 of the Act went still further to reinforce the congressional intent:[16]

> ... no restraining order or injunction shall be granted by any court of the United States ... in any case between an employer and employees, or between employers and employees, or between employees, or between persons employed and persons seeking employment, involving or growing out of, a dispute concerning terms or conditions of employment, unless necessary to prevent irreparable injury to property, or to a property right, ... for which injury there is no adequate remedy at law ...

In other words, no injunctions were to be issued against labor activities unless no other remedy existed. This section seemed to remove peaceful union activities from the threat of injunction. If a striker, for example, threw a brick through a plant window or caused other tangible property damage, there were obvious legal prohibitions and actions that could be taken against him. However, if he picketed peacefully outside the plant, the only damage was to the employer's *intangible* property (i.e., reputation, goodwill, etc.), and no injunction could be issued.

As if to be absolutely certain that the courts understood its message, Congress stated in Section 20 that no injunction or restraining order could be issued against individuals or groups for the following activities:

> ... terminating any relation of employment, or from ceasing to perform any work or labor [i.e., striking] or from recommending ... by peaceful means to do so; ... attending at any place where any such person or persons may lawfully be, for the purpose of peacefully obtaining or communicating information, or from peacefully persuading any person to work or to abstain from working [i.e., picketing] ... or from ceasing to patronize or employ any party to such dispute [i.e., primary boycott] ... or from paying or giving to, or withholding ... strike benefits ... or from peaceably assembling in a lawful manner ... nor shall any of the acts specified in this paragraph be considered or held to be violations of any law of the United States.

The first U.S. Supreme Court test of the Clayton Act came in the case of *Duplex Printing Press Company v. Deering* in 1921.[17] The International Mechanics' Union sought to organize the Duplex Company, which was the only nonunion manufacturer of printing presses. In order to place pressure on the company, members of the union throughout the nation refused to repair any Duplex presses or to work for anyone who owned a Duplex press. The majority of the Supreme Court upheld a lower court ruling that the union had violated the Sherman Act. In its curious opinion, the Court stated that (1) the Clayton Act did not substantially modify the Sherman Act but merely incorporated previous court rulings on unions and antitrust into it; (2) Section 6 did not authorize unions to act as conspiracies merely because it said that they were not; and (3) Section 20 limited judicial authority to issue injunctions only in labor disputes between an employer and his employees, and that none of the persons refusing to repair Duplex presses or to work for Duplex press owners were employees of the Duplex Company. In effect, the Court decided that Congress had done nothing by passage of the Clayton Act!

THE NORRIS-LA GUARDIA ACT: NEW RULES FOR THE OPPONENTS

Throughout the 1920s, the Supreme Court attempted to find some way to allow clearly peaceful union activities while rationalizing its past decisions.[18] However, there continued to be confusion in the law of collective bargaining, and the feeling persisted among many union leaders that a "double standard" existed with respect to the activities that management and unions were permitted to undertake. For these and other reasons, organized labor supported strongly the passage of legislation purportedly drafted by then Professor Felix Frankfurter (later Supreme Court Justice) that was designed to clarify the issues. Congress passed the Anti-Injunction or "Norris-La Guardia" Act in 1932.[19]

Section 3 of the Act outlawed the so-called "yellow dog" contracts under which workers agreed to abstain from union membership as a condition of continued employment. However, Section 4 dealt specifically with the matter of injunctions. It prohibited federal court issuance of any restraining order or temporary or permanent injunction in a labor dispute that would have the effect of preventing individuals or groups (e.g., unions) from striking, joining a union, obtaining strike benefits, giving legal assistance, publicizing a labor dispute, stating an intention to commit such acts, agreeing with other persons to commit such acts, or causing others to commit such acts. Section 5 eliminated finally the question of unions as conspiracies:

> No court of the United States shall have jurisdiction to issue a restraining order . . . or injunction upon the ground that any of the persons participating or interested in a labor dispute constitute or are engaged in an unlawful combination or conspiracy . . .

Section 6 removed from individual union members or officers any responsibility for the unlawful actions of other members or officers. Section 13 left no doubt about the meaning of "labor dispute" within the Act:

> . . . involves persons who are engaged in the same industry, craft, trade, or occupation; or who have direct or indirect interests therein; or who are employees of the same employer; or who are members of the same or an affiliated organization of employers or employees; whether such dispute is (1) between one or more employers or associations of employers and one or more employees or associations of employees; (2) between one or more employers or associations of employers; (3) between one or more employees or associations of employees and one or more employees or associations of employees . . .

By doing so, the Act destroyed most of the precedents in the *Loewe v. Lawlor* decision, including the prohibition on secondary boycotts. This legislation, in a sense, belongs to a different era from that which followed it. It was designed neither to promote nor to retard the growth of unionism. It required neither unions nor managements to accept or recognize one another. Instead, the Anti-Injunction Act permitted simply each party to use the same methods to achieve its ends unhampered by federal control and left the outcome of disputes to the relative skills and strengths of the parties.

THE WAGNER ACT AND THE NEW DEAL

The election of President Franklin Roosevelt and a Democratic Congress in 1932 brought with it sweeping and innovative legislation to aid economic recovery from depression and to provide better social services to the public. This legislation and the approach to government that it implied came to be known as the "New Deal." The first "New Deal" attempts to resolve labor-management relations problems and to guarantee to workers the right to organize were contained in the National Industrial Recovery Act, but that legislation was declared unconstitutional. Then, Senator Robert Wagner introduced legislation in 1935 to provide a comprehensive governmental system for the promotion of peaceful industrial relations within a context of the recognition of the right of employees to organize into unions of their own choosing.

Senator Wagner believed that the growth of so-called "company unions" represented a major impediment to the right of workers to choose a bargaining representative.[20] He also recognized some deficiencies in the system developed under the National Industrial Recovery Act from his service as chairman of the board that administered its labor provisions. For example, that legislation had given employees the right to organize and bargain collectively through representatives of their own choice but lacked any means for settlement of representation disputes or for compelling employers to recognize and bargain with such representatives. Wagner attempted to eliminate some earlier problems by specifying the provisions of his bill in some detail in order to avoid long legal confrontations and debates over interpretation. Senator Wagner's bill was passed with some modifications and signed into law on July 27, 1935, becoming the National Labor Relations Act (NLRA).

The NLRA begins with a statement that:[21]

> . . . the denial by some employers of the right of employees to organize and the refusal by some employers to accept the procedure of collective bargaining lead to strikes and other forms of industrial strife or unrest, which have the intent or necessary effect of burdening or obstructing commerce . . .

> The inequality of bargaining power between employees who do not possess full freedom of association or actual liberty of contract, and employers who are organized in the corporate or other forms of ownership association substantially burdens and affects the flow of commerce, and tends to aggravate recurrent business depressions by depressing wage rates and the purchasing power of wage earners in industry and by preventing the stabilization of competitive wage rates and working conditions . . .

In other words, the U.S. Congress had affirmed its support for the principle of collective bargaining and for the rights of workers to organize into unions for that purpose as a matter of public policy. The principle was affirmed strongly in the heart of the Act, Section 7:

> Employees shall have the right to self-organization, to form, join, or

assist labor organizations, to bargain collectively through representatives of their own choosing, and to engage in concerted activities for the purpose of collective bargaining or other mutual aid or protection.

Section 8 listed five "unfair labor practices" by employers which were delcared to be illegal. These were (1) interference, restraint, or coercion of employees in their exercise of Section 7 rights; (2) domination, interference, or support of employee organizations; (3) discrimination in hiring or tenure of employees in an effort to encourage or discourage union membership;[22] (4) discrimination against an employee for filing charges under the Act; and (5) refusal to bargain collectively with designated employee representatives.

Congress established the National Labor Relations Board (NLRB) in this legislation to administer its provisions. The original NLRB was composed of three members appointed by the President by and with the advice and consent of the Senate to alternate five-year terms plus any regional or other assistants that the NLRB might find necessary. The NLRB was empowered to conduct representation elections, determine appropriate bargaining units, and hear charges of violations of the Act. Its specific responsibilities are discussed in detail in later chapters.

There was a substantial body of legal opinion that felt that the Act would be declared unconstitutional. However, the U.S. Supreme Court upheld the constitutionality of the NLRA in *NLRB v. Jones and Laughlin Steel Corporation* in 1937.[23] The new NLRB prosecuted the NLRA provisions vigorously in its early years, assuming that its responsibilities were with the needs and desires of the workers and unions almost to the exclusion of the employers. The Board was supported increasingly by the courts in this outlook. Several judicial decisions will serve as examples of the changing judicial attitudes.

The case of *Apex v. Leader* involved a situation in which a union of hosiery workers was attempting to organize the remaining nonunion producers in an effort to eliminate nonunion competition.[24] A group of union members and company employees seized the Apex Company plant in Philadelphia by locking it up, doing damage to it, and refusing to let the company ship over 100,000 dozens of hosiery, most of which was for interstate sales. The company brought suit against the union under the Sherman Act and sought to have its actions enjoined. When the case ultimately reached the U.S. Supreme Court the ruling favored the union. The majority decision held that federal courts had no jurisdiction because all of the parties involved were Pennsylvania citizens; that the union was attempting simply to pressure the company into accepting union organization and not to control the hosiery market; and that the Sherman Act had never been used against this type of activity!

The case of *U.S. v. Hutcheson* involved a jurisdictional dispute between the Carpenters' and Machinists' unions over which should have the right to dismantling work at a St. Louis brewing company.[25] When the company awarded the work to members of the Machinists' union the Carpenters' union struck the company, picketed its plants, and asked union members not to purchase the firm's products through newspapers and circulars. Once again the U.S. Supreme Court refused to accept the union's actions as proof of violation of the Sherman Act, the majority declaring that the Clayton Act absolved such conduct, e.g., a secondary boycott, from prosecution under the Sherman Act.

This series of decisions reached a climax in the case of *Hunt v. Crumbock*.[26] In a previous strike some years earlier, a member of a truckers' union had been killed. His employer was tried and acquitted on a charge of murder. Later this union organized all of the trucking companies in the area and obtained an agreement from a large chain store to use only organized trucking companies. Then, although the employer in question wanted to bargain, the union refused to do so or to allow its members to work for him, alleging that he was a murderer. Therefore, although the employer had dealt with the chain stores for many years, he lost their business. The U.S. Supreme Court ruled in favor of the union.

These court decisions and what some observers considered a prounion bias of the NLRB combined with a series of disastrous postwar strikes that altered public opinion and the election of a Republican Congress in 1946 to produce a major alteration in labor law in the direction of what some considered a "righting of the balance."

THE TAFT-HARTLEY ACT: A BALANCED APPROACH

Congress passed the Labor-Management Relations (LMRA) or "Taft-Hartley" Act in 1947 as a series of amendments to the NLRA in an attempt to balance its provisions.[27] The law begins with a policy statement that says in part:

> It is the purpose and policy of this Act, in order to promote the full flow of commerce, to prescribe the legitimate rights of both employees and employers . . . to provide orderly and peaceful procedures for preventing the interference by either with the legitimate rights of the other, to protect the rights of individual employees in their relations with labor organizations . . . and to protect the rights of the public in connection with labor disputes affecting commerce.

Organized labor, with assistance from passage of the NLRA, the rise of the CIO, and the wartime conditions, had grown from a relatively small and ineffective group to a large and powerful factor in the economy. Therefore, Congress was expressing the view that organized labor could impede commerce just as corporations might.

Most provisions of the LMRA are discussed in detail in later chapters in the context of their practical effects on collective bargaining. Therefore, we shall only summarize the major points here. Provision was made for settlement of "national emergency" strikes or disputes. The Federal Mediation and Conciliation Service was created to attempt to settle disputes as a "third party" when called upon by one of the disputing parties.[28] Suits by either party to an agreement were permitted in federal courts for violation of the agreement. The secondary boycott, jurisdictional strikes, the closed shop, and strikes against the federal government were outlawed. States were permitted to pass legislation that outlaws the union shop. Anyone desiring to modify an existing collective bargaining agreement is required to notify the opposite party of his intention at least 60 days prior to the expiration of the agreement. A series of unfair labor practices by unions were added to those by management. These include restraint or coercion of employees or employers in their organizational rights, discrimination against an employee denied union membership for any reason other than nonpayment of dues, refusal to bargain collectively, the conduct of illegal strikes or boycotts,[29] the charging of excessive or discriminatory dues or fees under a union shop agreement, and the exacting of compensation for services not performed or to be performed.

THE LANDRUM-GRIFFIN ACT: THE COMING OF INTERNAL REGULATIONS

Hearings conducted by Senator McClellan in 1958 disclosed extensive abuses by a few unions of their responsibilities and their power. There were indications that some unions had denied their membership a full opportunity to participate in union affairs, had developed irregular relationships with employers, and had used their power to extract funds illegally.[30] As a result, Congress acted for the first time to extend governmental control to the *internal* activities of unions with passage of the Labor-Management Reporting and Disclosure Act of 1959, or "Landrum-Griffin" Act.[31]

Title I of the Act is called the "Bill of Rights of Members of Labor Organizations." It is designed to insure union members the right to participate fully in union elections, to be charged reasonable fees and dues, and to be protected against improper disciplines. Title II requires the filing of detailed annual reports by union and corporate officers and labor relations consultants on their financial activities. Title III limits the conditions under which an international union may exercise a trusteeship over its affiliated local unions. Title IV requires the maintenance of democratic safeguards in union elections. Title V denies the privilege of union office to persons convicted of certain crimes. Title VI contains a variety of miscellaneous provisions to be discussed in succeeding chapters.

SUMMARY

As unions have grown in size and strength, so too have the volume and detail of labor law. Unions have moved from a position of being considered conspiracies under the law to one of being recognized as an important factor for good or ill in the economy. There has been a steady progression from laws that merely "set the rules of the game" (Norris-La Guardia) to those which delineate the rights and responsibilities of the parties (Wagner and Taft-Hartley Acts) and finally to those which regulate the internal activities of the parties (Landrum-Griffin Act). The ways in which these laws affect the daily conduct of industrial relations by employers, unions, and employees will be considered in what follows.

IMPORTANT NEW TERMS INTRODUCED

Conspiracy doctrine: The legal doctrine that two or more workers could not engage in concerted economic activity designed to require their employer to satisfy their demands.

Injunction: A court order requiring the temporary ceasing of an activity, pending full judicial review. Violation of the order constitutes "contempt of court."

SUGGESTED ADDITIONAL READINGS

Bureau of National Affairs, *Major Labor-Law Principles Established by the NLRB and the Court* (issued periodically), is a compilation of the current status of labor law and its interpretations indexed according to the types of issue.

Milton Derber and Edwin Young (eds.), *Labor and the New Deal* (Madison: University of Wisconsin Press, 1961), does not deal specifically with labor law but provides interesting insights into the social and the economic issues surrounding the passage of much of the early legislation.

Marten S. Estey, Philip Taft, and Martin Wagner (eds.), *Regulating Union Government* (New York: Harper and Row, 1964), is concerned with various issues related to passage of the Labor-Management Reporting and Disclosures Act and its effects.

Charles O. Gregory, *Labor and the Law,* 2nd rev. ed. (New York: W. W. Norton, 1961) provides an excellent summary of various historical factors in the development of labor law and a detailed analysis of the more important cases.

The *Labor Relations Reporter* is a periodical published by the Bureau of National Affairs that offers current analysis of labor law decisions.

NOTES

[1] See Foster Rhea Dulles, *Labor in America* (New York: Thomas Y. Crowell, 1949), p. 11.

[2] Philip Taft, *Organized Labor in American History* (New York: Harper and Row, 1964), p. 5.

3 John R. Commons and Associates (eds.), *A Documentary History of American Industrial Society* (Cleveland: Arthur H. Clark, 1910), III, pp. 64-65.

[4] Ibid., p. 68.

[5] See Dulles, p. 29, and Walter Nelles, "The First American Labor Case," *Yale Law Journal* (December 1931), pp. 165-200.

[6] The closed shop refers to a collective bargaining agreement in which the employer agrees to hire only persons who are members of a given union.

[7] *Commonwealth v. Hunt,* 4 Metcalf, III (Mass., 1842).

[8] See *Report of the U.S. Strike Commission* (Washington: U.S. Government Printing Office, 1895) for further details on this strike.

[9] An injunction is a temporary prohibition against some actions by one or more persons, pending a hearing to determine whether the acts should be prohibited or "enjoined" permanently.

[10] For example, see Edward H. Chamberlin, "The Monopoly Power of Labor," in David McCord Wright (ed.), *The Impact of the Labor Union* (New York: Augustus M. Kelley, 1966), pp. 168-187; and Edward S. Mason, "Labor Monopoly and All That," *Annual Proceedings, Industrial Relations Research Association,* 1955, pp. 188-208.

[11] Act of July 2, 1890, 26 Stat. 209, Ch. 647, Secs. 1-8.

[12] *Loewe v. Lawlor,* 208 U.S. 274 (1908).

[13] A primary boycott involves the refusal of union members to purchase the products of a firm with whom the union has a dispute. By contrast, the secondary boycott involves refusal to deal with a firm with whom the given union has no dispute. In this case, for example, the union members had no labor dispute with the retailers.

[14] *American Federationist* (July 1914), p. 553.

[15] 38 Stat. 731 U.S. Code, Sec. 17.

[16] 38 Stat. 738, 29 U.S. Code, Sec. 52.

[17] *Duplex Printing Press Company v. Deering,* 254 U.S. 443 (1921).

[18] For example, see *United Mine Workers of America v. Coronado Coal Co.,* 259 U.S. 344 (1922).

[19] Act of March 23, 1932, 47 Stat. 70-73, Ch. 90, Secs. 1-15, Public Law 65, U.S. Code, Sec. 101-115.

[20] Company unions were employee organizations financed and dominated by employers that were used to inhibit the development of unions free of control by employers.

[21] Act of July 5, 1935, Ch. 372, 59 Stat. 449-457, Public Law 198, 29 U.S. Code, Secs. 151-166.

[22] An exception was made for the "closed shop" and "union shop." The latter refers to a situation in which a person must join the union within a specified time period after being hired or forfeit his employment.

[23] *NLRA v. Jones and Laughlin Steel Corporation,* 301 U.S. 1 (1937).

[24] *Apex Hosiery Company v. Leader,* 310 U.S. 469 (1940).

[25] *United States v. Hutcheson,* G1 Sup. Ct. 463, 312 U.S. 219 (1941).

[26] *Hunt v. Crumbock,* 325 U.S. 821 (1945).

[27] Act of June 23, 1947, Public Law 101.

[28] Unlike arbitration in which a binding award is made by the third party, mediation involves only the attempt by the third party to bring the other two together. Conciliation involves the recommendation of a compromise solution which is not binding by the third party.

[29] Illegal strikes or boycotts refer generally to those conducted when the collective bargaining agreement contains a "no-strike" pledge by the union.

[30] See *Final Report of the Select Committee on Improper Activities in the Labor or Management Field,* Senate Report 1139, 86th Cong., 2nd sess., 1960.

[31] Act of September 14, 1959, Public Law 86-257.

8

Collective Bargaining

THE NATIONAL LABOR RELATIONS BOARD

After a group of employees and/or a union has presented the National Labor Relations Board (NLRB) with evidence that a significant proportion of the employees at a company want a union to act as their agent for the purpose of collective bargaining, the NLRB will begin to prepare for a *representation election*.[1] First, the NLRB will determine the "appropriate bargaining unit," e.g., what is the proper group of employees for a given union to represent in collective bargaining if a union is selected by the workers. The appropriate unit may be a group of employees in the same department or shop, the same occupation or craft, the same type of work (i.e., "blue collar" or "white collar"), etc.[2]

Next, an NLRB representative decides which employees in the bargaining unit are eligible to vote in the election. This decision is made often by selecting a given pay day prior to the election and using the payroll list of employees in the bargaining unit on that day as the list of eligible voters. Third, the NLRB announces the place, date, and time of the election and assigns one or more of its representatives to conduct the election. A convenient polling place, often at the site of the business, is selected; and a secret ballot election is conducted with observers present from both management and the union. These observers may not campaign at the polling place but may challenge the eligibility of any voter.

Finally, the votes are counted in the presence of union and management representatives; and any "challenged" ballots are put aside to be counted only if their number might ultimately affect the outcome of the election, at which time a determination is made on each challenge. If one choice (e.g., union representation or no union) has a majority of the votes cast by employees and the challenged ballots could not affect the outcome, the NLRB either certifies the union as the bargaining agent for the group of employees or declares that employees have rejected union representation. If the majority of the voting employees in the bargaining unit oppose representation, the union must wait 12 months before seeking another election. If there are more than two choices on the ballot (two unions are contending for the right to represent the employees) and no choice receives a majority, the NLRB conducts a "run-off" election between the two choices receiving the most votes. In all cases, both union(s) and management have the right to ask that the decision be set aside and a new election conducted if they can prove[3] to the NLRB that an *unfair labor practice*[3] was committed. If the union is certified as the bargaining agent, collective bargaining between management and union representatives will begin. Each side is required to bargain collectively with the other.[4]

THE PROCESS AND THE PARTICIPANTS

Although the rigors of a hard-fought union organizing campaign may leave each side with suspicions, mistrust, and ill feelings toward the other, the parties will begin negotiations after the union is certified. These negotiations may take many forms depending largely on the nature and size of the firm and the union. In simplest form, there may be a meeting between the company and union presidents at a "neutral" site (e.g., a local fraternal order hall, restaurant, etc.) with each perhaps assisted by an attorney and provided with information from a trade association or international union respectively. In its most elaborate form, negotiations may involve 100 or more persons from the management of a large corporation and the official staff of several unions, each assisted by expert staff members who have spent a year or more on research in preparation for the negotiations. Subcommittees may be organized, perhaps even in advance of the negotiations, to formulate proposed contract clauses on specific subjects for consideration by the larger body.

However, most negotiations will assume a form somewhere between these two extremes. Although there is no "typical" or standard form, one can outline the general way in which such negotiations might develop. If there is already a contract in force, each party must notify the other of any intention to modify the agreement at least 60 days prior to the expiration of the agreement.[5] In the context of this discussion of an initial contract, this provision is obviously not applicable.

The parties will establish a mutually acceptable time and place at which to begin negotiations. The number of persons on the management and union bargaining committees will be a function of the size of the company and the scope and complexity of the negotiations. At a minimum, the management committee will probably include the industrial relations or personnel director (if the company is sufficiently large to have such an individual), a corporate officer empowered to make agreements, and counsel for the company who may be either a member of their legal staff or a labor relations attorney retained for this purpose. The union committee will probably include an elected officer, a business agent, if the local union is sufficiently large, and a representative from the international union to provide professional advice and to seek conformity of the local contract with the goals of the international union. The union may have counsel present either from the international union legal staff or an attorney retained for this purpose.

It is likely that the union will have held a local meeting prior to the start of negotiations for the purpose of establishing its bargaining demands. At such a meeting, the local union members ratify, reject, or amend the proposals developed by their officers or by a bargaining committee.[6] Advice on these proposals may have been obtained from the international union's research department. Company officials have probably prepared their offers in advance also, using available data on wages, hours, etc., that may have been supplied by their trade or industry association or by their personnel or industrial relations staff. It is these initial demands by the union and offers by the company that are presented during the opening negotiation sessions.

The parties may select a chairman to conduct the sessions; and each party may select an official spokesman. At this point, the bargaining commences. Issues that are easy to resolve or on which there seems to be a mutuality of opinion will likely be considered first with other, more complex or difficult issues postponed. The union may initially seek far more than it expects to obtain and the company initially offer far less than it expects to concede in the realization that concessions from the original position may be necessary later. Sessions will recess at various intervals to permit each side to caucus and discuss demands or offers.

If agreement proves impossible to reach on one or more issues, the assistance of a state or federal mediator may be sought (see below) to provide the view of an outside "third party" who may be able to resolve the differences or propose an acceptable compromise. Should this procedure fail to achieve an agreement the result may be a strike if the union members feel strongly enough on the issue(s) to support such an action. Members will refuse to report for work. Picket lines will be established at the company to inform the public of the dispute, to alert other union members to the dispute, and to discourage other workers from entering the place of business. Boycotts of the firm's products may be sought with the cooperation of other unions. The employer may attempt to operate his firm with management personnel or replacements or (more likely) will simply close his operations. Negotiations may continue during the strike or resume at some point if they have ceased. With rare exceptions, one side or both will find continuation of the strike situation too costly in terms of lost profits and/or wages and will agree to settle the disputed issues.

When agreement is reached finally it is reduced to writing and submitted to the union membership for ratification. If ratified by a majority of the members voting, it becomes valid until its expiration date or until one or more sections may be "reopened."[7]

THE AGREEMENT

The collective bargaining agreement or the contract to which the parties have agreed becomes the document on which the firm must base its industrial relations policies and actions. It describes the rights and responsibilities of the employees, the employer, and the union and its staff. Obviously the complexity and length of agreements vary considerably from a few pages of simple paragraphs to several hundred pages of highly detailed clauses relating to every aspect of the employer-employee relationship, depending on the size of the establishment. As with the description of the collective bargaining process, we can provide here only a generalized description of the more common features of such agreements.

Union Recognition

A typical agreement begins with a section stating that the firm recognizes the particular union as the exclusive bargaining representative for all or certain groups of its employees.[8] Such a section reaffirms that the employees have selected the union to represent them on all matters covered by the agreement and prevents the firm from dealing with other unions or with the employees directly and in the absence of union presence. The union must be consulted on matters covered by the agreement. This section will also identify groups of employees not covered by the agreement.[9] Some agreements include a clause in this section to explain what happens to union recognition if a change in ownership of the firm occurs.

Union Security

There are various forms of "union security," a term given to arrangements that require some form of union membership by a firm's employees in the bargaining unit. The agreement may require that all persons hired into the bargaining unit become union members after the completion of a probationary period of, most commonly, 30, 60, or 90 days. Failure to join the union after that period results in the dismissal of the employee. However, he is usually protected by the provisions of the agreement during this period and is placed on the seniority list (see below) upon completion of it. This form of union security is called the *union shop* and represents the most common type.[10]

Another form of union security is called *maintenance of membership* under which an employee is not required to join the union as a condition of retaining his employment but must remain in the union once he becomes a member. An *agency shop* does not require an employee to join the union but obligates him to pay the equivalent of dues to the union. The rationale given by proponents of this form of union security is that the union, under the law, must represent all employees, and, therefore, all employees should share in the cost of this representation.

A system of dues collection called the "checkoff" may be included in the union security section if the employer agrees. When there is such a system the employer agrees to deduct from the members' monthly paychecks an amount equal to their union dues and to give this money to the union. Some states require that employees authorize such deductions in writing.

Union Business

Most agreements contain provisions that relate to the ways in which union representatives may perform their contractual duties. Authorized representatives may be accorded access to the offices and plant of the firm and the right to examine company employment records. Shop stewards may be allowed to process grievances and to conduct union business during working hours while being paid their normal wages as employees by the company. Other agreements may simply provide released time without pay. Often this time, whether compensated or not, is limited to a fixed number of hours per week or other convenient time period. Limitations on the authority of stewards to engage in disruption of the company's operations are usually contained in the agreement.

Seniority

Most agreements contain provisions on promotions and reductions in the work force that are referred to as "seniority" clauses. Generally these clauses require the firm to announce any job vacancy and to give employees the right to apply or "bid" for the job on the basis of their tenure with the company. The vacant job may be attractive because of its wage rate, the shift on which it occurs, its demands, etc. These clauses usually require that, if all other factors are equal, the employee seeking the job who has been employed the longest time shall receive it.[11] Similarly, reductions in the work force are made in reverse order of seniority. The length of time that constitutes seniority may be the employee's tenure with the company or his tenure in a particular department.

Wages, Hours, and Fringe Benefits

The agreement may contain a series of job classifications and either a wage rate or range of wage rates for each one. If there are differentials in wages for work on various shifts, these will be specified. Overtime or work beyond some weekly number of hours (usually 40, which is the legal limit) or work on holidays or weekends is rewarded with additional pay (frequently 1.5 or 2.0 times the normal rate). The agreement will specify these differentials.

The agreement may include various types of "fringe benefits." These are rewards of employment other than wages and include, among others, employer- and/or employer-employee-financed medical benefits, insurance, pensions, sick leave, vacations, and supplementary unemployment benefits. The agreement will specify such benefits in detail.

There is an increasing tendency toward the inclusion of a "cost of living" clause. Under such an agreement, employees are given a wage increase when the Consumers' Price Index of the U.S. Department of Labor increases by a given amount. These increases are usually computed at intervals of 6 months or one year after the effective date of the agreement.

Either in this section or elsewhere, most agreements include statements about the discharge of employees. These will specify the conditions under which an employee may be discharged, often including a provision that requires the employer to substantiate "just cause" and providing an appeal mechanism for the employee and/or his union. The section may include provision for severance pay.[12]

TRENDS IN COLLECTIVE BARGAINING

Today nearly 30 percent of nonagricultural workers in the U.S. labor force are covered by a collective bargaining agreement. The percentages of workers organized into unions and covered by agreements vary widely among geographic regions, occupations, and industries. However, the one factor common to all of these varied collective bargaining relationships is change. Each labor-management relationship involves a continuing evolution and refinement with the aim of providing the parties with more efficient means of dealing with one another. Several changes or trends in collective bargaining that are receiving attention from both interested practitioners and students of industrial relations are discussed below.

Coordinated Bargaining

There are many employers who bargain with more than one union, perhaps ten or more in extreme cases. This situation may exist because a multi-plant company has a separate agreement with each union at each of its plants or because a given plant may include several bargaining units (i.e., maintenance, production, and clerical employees) each represented by a different union. In some instances, employers have bargained separately with each union and/or with the individual local unions at each plant, selecting the weakest union to bargain with first in order to obtain a favorable settlement that might "set a pattern" for subsequent negotiations with the other unions.

In recent years, some unions have attempted to combat this tactic by engaging in mutual action under the auspices of the AFL-CIO Industrial Union Department (IUD) which serves as a coordinating agent. One approach has involved the establishment by the IUD of a committee of representatives for all of the unions that negotiate with a given company. Through such a committee, information and experiences are exchanged. Alternatively, each union may attempt to have observers at the negotiations involving each other union. A second approach involves the agreement by the international presidents of all concerned unions to determine jointly their demands and to negotiate as a group with the employer. The emergence of more "conglomerate" firms with holdings in many industries may accelerate this trend.[13]

Adjustment to Technological Change

The increased pace in the introduction of "automation" or labor-saving technologies has posed a dilemma for the collective bargaining participants. Both parties have come to recognize that technological innovation may be necessary to make firms competitive within their industry and, increasingly, with foreign firms in, the world market, and thus to avoid the loss of jobs inherent in decreased sales of their products. However, these innovations may involve the displacement of some workers or even of large numbers of workers if the innovation requires construction of a new plant in a different location. Often these displaced workers will encounter great difficulty in obtaining new employment, particularly if they lack an easily transferable skill or if alternative job opportunities are limited in their communities.

Realizing their responsibilities to workers who may become displaced, both unions and managements in various industries have sought cooperative approaches to the solution of this dilemma instead of the unilateral exercise of prerogatives by management or blind opposition to change by unions that characterized some past situations. The simplest cooperative solution is the inclusion in the agreement of a requirement that management consult with the union before the introduction of labor-saving technologies. The employer may be encouraged to institute reductions in the work force through attrition (e.g., workers who retire or resign are not replaced) rather than through layoffs. There are examples of managements and unions that have established elaborate plans to ease the personal effects of technological change.

One example is a 1961 agreement between Armour and Company, which was relocating many of its operations, and two unions in the meat-packing industry with whom it bargained that established a plan to diminish the personal hardships associated with plant closings. The company agreed to establish an Automation Fund to finance the plan and to be administered by a tripartite committee composed of company, union, and public members. Armour agreed to provide a 90 days' notice of plant closings, to staff its new plants substantially with displaced workers from closed plants, and to assist displaced workers desiring to move to new plants with their relocation expenses. Workers about to be displaced could "bump" or displace less senior workers at existing plants or move to new plants. Early retirement benefits were made attractive for older workers. Generous severance pay arrangements and opportunities for retraining were provided for displaced workers desiring to leave Armour employment.[14]

A 1962 agreement between the Kaiser Steel Corporation and the United Steelworkers of America established a Long Range Sharing Plan to protect employees against the loss of jobs or income because of the introduction of new technology.[15] Although workers could be displaced because of reduced sales, no worker could lose his job because of technological change. Displaced workers are put in vacant jobs in the plant and paid the less of 40 hours' weekly pay or pay for the average workweek in the plant. If forced to accept lower paying jobs, workers receive an allowance equal to the differential for up to three years. In addition, 32.5 percent of the savings in materials or labor cost by the company is used to finance the above arrangements with any excess being distributed as bonuses to the employees, some of which have been substantial.

The Armour and Kaiser plans are but two, rather well-publicized, examples of many such agreements. The Bureau of Labor Statistics found in 1969 that 21.5 percent of the 1,823 agreements that they studied had clauses on plant relocation which covered over 2.9 million workers.[16] Nearly one-third of the agreements studied contained provisions for the protection of covered workers required or requesting transfer to another plant or company.[17] Among these provisions were 34.5 percent which require the company to pay all or a part of the cost of relocation.[18]

Cost-of-living Clauses

There is nothing new about cost-of-living or so-called "escalator" clauses as they were called in the years following World War II when they became widespread. Unions have sought continually to mitigate adverse effects on their members' real incomes that might result from long-term agreements during the period of which the cost of living might increase. One approach has been to build into the agreement a series of deferred wage increases or "step" increases to take effect over the life of the agreement. The alternative approach of cost-of-living clauses under which wages are increased during the life of the agreement automatically as the Consumers' Price Index increases became popular after General Motors and the United Automobile Workers negotiated such an agreement in 1948. Unions could negotiate long-term agreements without jeopardizing their members' real incomes; and managements could negotiate less frequently and anticipate labor cost increases. Rapid price increases caused by the Korean conflict increased the popularity of cost-of-living provisions, and nearly 4 million workers were covered by such agreements by

1957.[19] After 1959, such provisions became less popular and only 1.8 million workers were covered by such agreements in 1963. In their place came various forms of deferred wage increases and emphases on other provisions of agreements, such as fringes, early retirement, etc.

The situation changed beginning with the announcement in 1971 of "Phase I" and "Phase II" economic controls by President Nixon and accelerated with inflation following removal of controls, with the result of a reversion to earlier thinking by union leaders and members. The fear that wages might become "frozen" for several years has provoked new interest in cost-of-living clauses. Related to this change is the announced policy of several major unions to negotiate only short-term agreements in order to protect their members' wages.

FEDERAL MEDIATION AND CONCILIATION SERVICE

Although the federal government, through the Department of Labor, had been involved in mediation and conciliation since 1913, it was not until 1947 that the Labor-Management Relations Act authorized the creation of an independent agency, the Federal Mediation and Conciliation Service. The legislation encouraged labor and management to use mediation and voluntary arbitration to avoid work stoppages, established a labor-management advisory panel for the Service, and required the parties to notify one another of the desire for changes in an agreement 60 days before its expiration. In addition to assisting the parties in the selection of arbitrators from the private sector, the FMCS employs staff to mediate disputes between unions and management. Working without formal authority, these individuals attempt to bring together the negotiators from both sides when requested. They have compiled an admirable record. In fiscal 1968, federal mediators participated in an average of 700 labor relations conferences weekly and assisted in the achievement of settlements without a strike in 107 of 145 actively mediated settlements.[20] A total of over 18,000 cases involved the FMCS that year.

IMPORTANT NEW TERMS INTRODUCED

Bargaining unit: A group of employees who, in the judgment of the National Labor Relations Board, have sufficiently common occupational, industrial, or other work characteristics to constitute an appropriate unit to be represented by a union for collective bargaining.

Unfair labor practice: An action by an employer or union which violates the intent of the National Labor Relations Act, as amended. Such actions are specified in the Act and its amendments.

Union security: A provision of a labor-management agreement which requires either union membership or the payment of union dues as a condition of continued employment.

Seniority: A term applied to provisions of agreements which require that length of employment be considered in promotions and layoffs.

SUGGESTED ADDITIONAL READINGS

Neil W. Chamberlain and James W. Kuhn, *Collective Bargaining,* 2nd ed. (New York: McGraw-Hill, 1965) offers a comprehensive description of collective bargaining and the administration of agreements.

Harold W. Davey, *Contemporary Collective Bargaining,* 3rd ed. (Englewood Cliffs: Prentice-Hall, 1972) is an excellent source of up-to-date information on the many aspects of collective bargaining.

NOTES

[1] This evidence is supplied usually in the form of cards signed by at least 30 percent of the eligible employees which indicate that they desire union representation, i.e., through the use of "authorization cards." It is possible for the employer to recognize the union on the basis of signed cards from a majority of the employees, but this form of recognition occurs infrequently.

[2] In determining the appropriate unit, the NLRB considers the history of collective bargaining, the employees' interests and desires, and the interchangeability of the employees.

[3] Both parties, for example, are prohibited from attempting to coerce or threaten employees in their choice by the National Labor Relations Act, as amended.

[4] The National Labor Relations Act, as amended, requires both parties to bargain collectively and imposes penalties for an unfair labor practice of failure to bargain. The employer is required to make genuine counterproposals to any union demands that he rejects, although they need not constitute concessions [see *Majure Transport Co. v. NLRB* (CA-5, 1952) 22 Labor Cases]. He is considered not to be bargaining in good faith if he, for example:

a. Makes concessions to the employees while union negotiations are in progress

b. Rejects union demands on subjects such as wages without a counter-proposal

c. Refuses to put the agreement into writing.

See U.S. Department of Labor, *Federal Labor Laws and Programs* (Washington: U.S. Government Printing Office, 1971).

[5] Such notification is required under the Labor-Management Relations Act which amended the National Labor Relations Act in 1947.

[6] It is likely that the union officials or bargaining committee may have asked for a strike vote at the meeting also. In essence, the members are asked whether they are willing to strike for their demands. Armed with such a

vote, the union negotiators may have a stronger position in the bargaining.

[7] Some contracts, particularly those which extend for several years, contain provisions that allow one or both parties to renegotiate or "reopen" various clauses after a specified period of time has elapsed. Wages are usually in this category.

[8] "Exclusive bargaining representative" means that the company recognizes that the particular union will be the only agent of its employees in the bargaining unit.

[9] Such exclusions would include supervisory personnel, confidential secretaries, and guards who are exempted by the Labor-Management Relations Act and subsequent judicial decisions as well as employees represented by any other union.

[10] The Labor-Management Relations Act outlawed the "closed shop" under which an individual was required to be a union member as a condition of obtaining employment. It permits individual states to outlaw the union shop with so-called "right-to-work" laws. Eighteen states have such laws.

[11] The agreement may be quite explicit in its definition of "equal qualifications," may leave the determination of equality to the parties, or may give the company the right to decide with the right to protest or register an exception through the grievance procedure given to the union.

[12] Severance pay is an amount of wages, commonly equivalent to one week's pay, which a discharged or laid-off employee receives to sustain himself during his search for new employment.

[13] The views of organized labor, management, and an academician, respectively on coordinated bargaining are presented in David Lasser, "Coordinated Bargaining: A Union Point of View"; Earl L. Engle, "Coordinated Bargaining: A Snare and a Delusion"; and George Hildebrand, "Coordinated Bargaining: An Economist's Point of View," in *Proceedings of the 1968 Annual Spring Meeting, Industrial Relations Research Association*, pp. 512-529.

[14] For details on one Armour experience, see Edwin Young, "The Armour Experience: A Case Study in Plant Shutdown," Gerald Somers, Edward Cushman, and Nat Weinberg (eds.), *Adjusting to Technological Change* (New York: Harper and Row, 1963), pp. 145-158.

[15] A description of this plan is contained in Bureau of Labor Statistics, *Recent Collective Bargaining and Technological Change*, BLS Report No. 266, March 1964 (Washington: U.S. Government Printing Office, 1964), p. 3.

[16] Bureau of Labor Statistics, *Major Collective Bargaining Agreements: Plant Movement, Transfer, and Relocation Allowances*, Bulletin No. 1425-10, July 1969 (Washington: U.S. Government Printing Office, 1969), p. 4.

[17] Ibid., p. 22.

[18] Ibid., p. 55.

[19] Bureau of Labor Statistics, *Major Collective Bargaining Agreements: Deferred Wage Increase and Escalator Clauses*, Bulletin No. 1425-4, January 1966 (Washington: U.S. Government Printing Office, 1966), p. 3.

[20]"Report on FMCS Mediation, Arbitration in Fiscal 1968," Bureau of National Affairs, *Labor Relations Yearbook 1969* (Washington: Bureau of National Affairs, 1970), p. 675.

9

Administration of the Agreement

Once a collective bargaining agreement has been reached, the parties must begin the larger (and perhaps more important) task of administering it. The union and management representatives strive to make their agreement a "living" document through this process. In order to do so, both parties adopt procedures for handling the daily problems that arise and through which their agreement is refined. This refinement will occur through applications and interpretations of the various clauses of the agreement rather than through changes in its wording. The procedure which facilitates this refinement is known as the *grievance procedure*. Therefore, this chapter will consider grievance procedure and its usual last step, final and binding arbitration.

IMPORTANCE OF GRIEVANCE PROCEDURE

The arbitrary exercise of power by industrial managers is limited once a union wins recognition. The unilateral power structure characteristic of a firm before union recognition is replaced with a bilateral power structure. Thus, the recognition of a union as the bargaining agent for a firm's employees introduces a system of industrial jurisprudence into administration. The implementation of this system occurs through the grievance procedure.

The grievance procedure is so inherent in the workings of any system of industrial justice that it has been called the "heart" of the agreement between a firm and a union. Moreover, the spread of formal grievance and arbitration procedures is a major characteristic of postwar collective bargaining (Table 1).[1] Although this may seem a generalization, examination of the essence of the grievance procedure offers some insight into both importance and rapid growth of its use.

TABLE 1
Grievance Procedure Provisions in Major
Collective Bargaining Agreements,
By Industry

	Number Studied		Number with Grievance Procedures		Number without Grievance Procedures	
Industry	*Agreements*	*Workers*	*Agreements*	*Workers*	*Agreements*	*Workers*
All Industry	1,717	7,438.4	1,697	7,387.7	20	50.8
Manufacturing	1,405	4,351.3	1,041	4,343.2	4	8.2
Nonmanufacturing	672	3,087.1	656	3,044.5	16	42.6

Source: U.S. Department of Labor, *Major Collective Bargaining Agreements: Grievance Procedures,* Bulletin No. 1425-1, 1964.

The essence of the procedure is that an employee, without jeopardizing his job, can complain about his working conditions and obtain a fair hearing at progressively higher levels of management. Four features are related to this concept:[2]

> First, the collective bargaining contract, . . . may create a source of grievances and disagreements through ambiguities of language and omissions, as do changing circumstances and violations. Second, the union is recognized and accepted as the spokesman for the aggrieved worker, and an inability to agree on a resolution of the issue becomes a dispute between union and management. Third, because an unresolved grievance becomes a union-management dispute, a way ultimately must be found to reach settlements short of a strike or lockout or substitutes for such action. Fourth, the process of adjusting grievances and grievance disputes is itself defined in the agreement, and . . . tends to become increasingly formal.

The preceding discussion illustrates the utility of the grievance procedure to the union, the firm, and the individual worker. The procedure is important to the worker for two basic reasons. First, it gives him the right, supported by the collective agreement, to express discontent about his work or the conditions under which he works. Second, the grievance procedure provides the worker with a means through which his discontent can be transmitted to successively higher levels of management with the assurance of receiving an answer. This communicative aspect of the grievance procedure is crucial to its utility to the worker because it is not enough simply to have the right to express a feeling of discontent.

For the union and the firm who negotiate the basic labor agreement, the grievance procedure provides the even greater utility of a legitimate means for settlement of the many unforeseeable problems likely to develop during the life of the agreement. Therefore, through the grievance adjustment process, the parties will possess a basic agreement which becomes more than a mere codification of inflexible terms and conditions of employment. In effect, the parties employ the grievance procedure to transform their agreement into a "living" document which is continually refined as new problems develop in day-to-day operations of the firm.

Robert Dubin has summarized this crucial aspect of the grievance procedure for day-to-day problems settlement as follows:[3]

> A grievance procedure expresses the realization that problems may arise in the future for which no solution can be specified in advance. Because a business enterprise is dependent on a group of operating personnel, it is recognized that each individual participant may, at some future date, become dissatisfied with his participation in the enterprise and seek redress short of transfer or resignation. It is impossible to so detail personnel rules in company policies and collective bargaining agreements that they cover all variations of any employee problem. The grievance procedure makes decisions possible in situations not covered by existing rules.

Mr. Justice Douglas added credence to Dubin's comments in the opinion of the U.S. Supreme Court in *United Steelworkers of America v. Warrior Gulf Navigation Company:*[4]

> Apart from matters that the parties specifically exclude, all of the questions on which the parties disagree must therefore come within the scope of the grievance and arbitration provisions of the collective agreement. The grievance procedure is, in other words, a part of the continuous collective bargaining process.

The preceding discussions have concerned the importance of the grievance procedure; we turn now to the method through which the process becomes operable.

PROCEDURE STEPS

The grievance procedure is a formal system of appeals. Therefore, some method must be used to ensure that a worker's expression of discontent will move automatically to the next, higher level when a settlement is not reached. To accomplish this, most collective bargaining agreements outline the various appeal stages by stating the steps through which the appeal shall proceed from its inception to ultimate settlement—through arbitration by a third party, if necessary.

The degree of formality in the steps through which an unresolved grievance progresses will vary with plant size, type of industry, or a multiplicity of other factors. Therefore, it is difficult to portray a "typical" grievance procedure and the interrelationship of the steps within it. However, we can describe the grievance procedures of agreements in a large (over 1,000 employees) and a small (fewer than 150 employees) firm as illustrations.

The grievance process in the agreement between *The Paper Box Manufacturers* and the *United Paperworkers International Union* illustrates the former. The various steps of this process are:[5]

> Any employee may discuss a grievance with the foreman prior to taking up said grievance with the union shop steward. Any meetings or conferences pertaining to grievances shall require the presence of the union shop steward and/or committee. Should differences arise in the plant between the company and the union or its members employed by the company or should any local trouble of any kind arise in the plant, such grievances shall be reported by the union shop steward to the superintendent or manager of the plant in writing. If the manager, or superintendent, union shop steward, and the party with the grievance are unable to arrive at a satisfactory settlement within 48 hours, the question shall then be referred to the owner of the company and the international president or accredited representatives, or the representative of Local 286, and they shall attempt to bring about a harmonious settlement, but if the above group is unable to come to a satisfactory conclusion within 48 hours, the management of the company and the international union shall each select a representative. These two shall choose a third. If the third arbitrator shall be selected under the rules of the American Arbitration Association, and these three shall constitute an arbitration board, . . . their findings shall be final and binding.

Similarly, the grievance process in the agreement between *Thorofare Markets, Inc.,* and the *International Brotherhood of Teamsters, Chauffeurs, Warehousemen and Helpers of America* illustrates the type found in agreements that cover small numbers of employees. The relevant steps of this procedure are:[6]

a. It is agreed that all grievances shall be presented to the employer in writing by the steward, signed by the employee who has the grievance. In the event of any differences or complaints over the interpretation or application of the terms of this agreement, they may become the subject of conference as follows:

1. Between the steward and the warehouse superintendent or his designated alternate.

2. In the event of further differences in adjusting the grievance, the union business agent or president shall discuss it with the warehouse superintendent.

3. In the event of further differences in seeking a mutually satisfactory settlement, the complaint will be discussed by the union president with the president of the company, or a designated administrative executive in the event of his absence.

4. Should this meeting fail in settling the item in question, either of the parties hereto may request arbitration.

ARBITRATION

The grievance procedure has been successful as an instrument for the peaceful resolution of labor and management problems. It has been so successful, in fact, that the vast majority of problems that arise from interpretation or application of the contract are settled between the parties themselves. This result promotes and fosters healthy management-union relationships. However, not all issues in a dispute can be resolved by the two parties. For one reason or another, one party may not agree with the other's interpretation or application of the contract. An apparent stalemate exists because each party feels his position is the right one. Discussion could end and resolution occur through a show of economic strength, i.e., a strike.

Most grievance procedures provide a final step, arbitration, to prevent the occurrence of such a situation. Arbitration allows the parties to submit their dispute to an impartial third party and to eliminate any threat to a continuation of production. Although most agreements restrict the arbitrators' decisions to application and interpretation of the agreement, their decisions are final and binding upon the parties.

The following provision from the agreement between *H. K. Porter Company* and the *International Brotherhood of Electrical Workers* is typical:[7]

> Any "arbitrable grievance," . . . which is not settled or disposed of under the Grievance Procedure, . . . may, at the request of either the Union or the Company, be submitted to an arbitrator. The decision of the arbitrator shall be final and binding upon the Company, the Union, and the Employees covered under this Agreement, so long as the

Arbitrator's decision does not exceed the scope and provisions of this Agreement and the grievance submission made to him.

Today, there is an almost universal acceptance of arbitration as the final step in the grievance procedure. The fact is surprising when one considers that only a very small percentage of all agreements contained such a provision in 1930. The decisions of the National War Labor Board during World War II led to its rapid acceptance.[8] Thus, arbitration provisions were included in 73 percent of all collective agreements by 1944. Currently, the provision for arbitration of some or all grievance disputes is contained in 94 percent of all collective agreements.[9] (See Table 2)

Types of Arbitration

In the United States, in contrast to most European countries, unsettled grievances are submitted to a neutral third party, i.e., his selection and remuneration are joint actions of the parties. Since these third-party arbitrators settle thousands of unresolved grievances each year, an examination of the subject matter of arbitrable disputes will provide useful insights on the arbitrator's duties. We can use the subject matter of disputes to classify the types of arbitration cases.

There are three basic types of dispute which an arbitrator may be requested to settle, namely, (1) *interest disputes*, (2) *jurisdictional disputes* (3) *grievance or interpretation disputes*. The differences between these three types are more than a mere matter of degree. This fact is well documented in the following passage from a major publication on arbitration:

> These three types of arbitration differ greatly in major and minor respects—the authority of the arbitrator, the scope of actual possible cases, their meaning in terms of the basic prerogatives of management and union, the range of problems set before the arbitrator, the influence of arbitrators upon labor management relations, etc.[10]

Grievance Arbitration. The most frequent type of arbitration (and the one with which the bulk of this chapter is concerned) is that involving the settlement of grievance or interpretation disputes. The most representative issues are those involving the interpretation, application, or alleged violation of the agreement. These issues can be included in the arbitration process for several reasons. First, the arbitrator can study the language of the relevant contract clause(s) in relation to the original statement of the grievance: thus he can determine whether the facts of the grievance are related to the agreement. Additionally, he can determine whether there are any precedents that have been established in the application of the clause in question.[11] Finally, he has the right to question the parties concerning their intentions when they were negotiating the agreement.

Negotiation Arbitration. Although most parties have accepted griev-ance arbitration as a method of achieving industrial peace, quite the opposite is true of negotiation (or contract) arbitration. This major aspect of union-management relations has not changed significantly since the pre-World War II era. Despite increasing governmental and public efforts in this direction, unions and managements have remained adamant in their resistance to arbitration of new contract clauses. Today, less than 2 percent of all major agreements provide for the arbitration of disputes involving new contract terms.[12] As noted elsewhere, mediation, not arbitration, is the more common method of avoiding work stoppage over new contract disputes.

When we consider that the issues in new contract negotiations involve wage rates, hours of work, and conditions of work, it is not surprising to find the parties reluctant to submit such issues to an outsider. An additional problem inherent here is the lack of subjective criteria on which to base an arbitration decision. Such difficult and controversial problems should be resolved by the parties themselves.

Jurisdictional Arbitration. Unlike grievance or negotiation arbitration jurisdictional arbitration is common in only one industry, construction. Nearly 70 percent of the contracts in this industry provide some procedure for the settlement of disputes between two unions over performance of a certain type of work. The impetus behind such widespread acceptance of arbitration over work-assignment disputes stems from Section 8(b)(4) of the Taft-Hartley Act. Under the terms of this section, ultimate determination of these disputes will be made by the National Labor Relations Board (NLRB) if the disputants fail to settle by themselves. Evidently, the disputants have wanted to avoid NLRB intervention because relatively few construction-industry jurisdictional disputes have been referred to it.

Regardless of the particular motivation behind acceptance of jurisdic-tional arbitration, it has been very effective. Before its advent, a minor work assignment dispute could easily result in a strike. Such a strike might create stoppage of an entire construction project. The employer, caught between two rival unions, would be helpless. Therefore, the employer is protected and industrial peace is preserved by allowing the dispute to go to arbitration.

Substantive Law on Arbitration

Other than the experiences of the War Labor Board, the Congress of the United States avoided any involvement in labor-management disputes involving specific enforcement of contracts until 1947. By passing the Labor-Management Relations Act of 1947, however, Congress substantially changed its posture. One section of the Act (Section 301) provided for Federal Court jurisdiction in contract violation and for enforcement suits.[13] Thus, the principle was established that a labor agreement is legally enforceable.

TABLE 2
Selection of Arbitrator and Agency Specified in Selected Major Collective Bargaining Agreements, 1961-62

(workers in thousands)

Method of selecting the arbitrator	Total		AAA		FMCS		Public agencies other than FMCS[1]		Two agencies or more[2]		Others[3]	
	Agreements	Workers	Agreements	Workers	Agreements	Workers	Agreements	Workers	Agreements	Workers	Agreements	Workers
Number studied	416	2,600.1										
Participation by outside agency or party	291	1,242.8	124	488.9	125	442.9	31	265.9	9	27.2	2	18.0
Arbitrator selected by:												
Company and union	230	1,085.2	86	387.8	112	411.2	25	246.0	6	23.4	1	17.0
From a list submitted by an outside agency	21	158.0	12	118.3	8	29.7	1	10.0	—	—	—	—
If unable to agree on arbitrator, from list submitted by outside agency[4]	89	467.2	18	47.8	65	224.9	5	193.3	1	1.3	—	—

112

table 2 cont.

If unable to agree on arbitrator, outside agency selects	120	460.0	56	221.7	39	156.6	19	42.7	5	22.1	1	17.0
Outside agency or party	48	116.9	29	65.2	12	30.5	6	20.0	1	1.2	—	—
In accordance with AAA rules	7	13.8	7	13.8	—	—	—	—	—	—	—	—
Others[5]	6	27.0	2	22.2	1	1.2	—	—	2	2.6	1	1.0
No outside agency specified—company and union select arbitrator[6]	125	1,357.3	—	—	—	—	—	—	—	—	—	—

[1] Includes 20 agreements which specified a state or city mediation agency; 10 which specified a federal or state judge; and one which named the Secretary of Labor.

[2] Includes five agreements which names the FMCS and AAA; and four which named the FMCS and a state mediation agency.

[3] One agreement with several permanent arbitrators named a private individual to select a replacement if the company and union were unable to agree in event of a vacancy; the other agreement was not clear.

[4] Includes four agreements which provided for selection by the outside agency if the parties were unable to agree after requesting a list.

[5] Includes one agreement in which method of selection was not clear; two which varied in different plants; and three which permitted the company and union to either select the arbitrator or call upon an outside agency.

[6] Includes seven agreements which did not mention how the arbitrator was selected.

Note: Because of rounding, sums of individual items may not equal total.

Source: U.S. Department of Labor, *Arbitration Procedures*, Bulletin No. 142 5-6, 1966.

Beginning in 1957 with the famous *Lincoln Mills* case and continuing into 1960 with the three *Steelworker* cases (better known as the *Trilogy*), the federal courts used Section 301 to clarify various questions on the arbitrability of grievances. Through these cases, the Supreme Court has significantly affected the position of arbitration and greatly increased its power and prestige.

Due to their length, a detailed treatment of each case will not be attempted. However, we can briefly summarize their significant effects on the scope of the arbitration process. In the first case, *Textile Workers Union of America v. Lincoln Mills,* the Court established that it was empowered to compel specific performance of arbitration clauses contained in collective agreements. Furthermore, in emphasizing the role of a no-strike clause the Court stated in part that:[14]

> . . . the agreement to arbitrate grievance disputes is the *quid pro quo* for an agreement not to strike. Viewed in this light, the legislation does more than confer jurisdiction in the federal courts over labor organizations. It expresses a federal policy that federal courts should enforce these agreements on behalf of or against labor organizations and that industrial peace can be best obtained only in that way.

Following the *Lincoln Mills* case, several cases involving the arbitrability of grievances further enhanced the status of arbitration. These are the *Trilogy* decisions which were handed down by the Supreme Court on June 20, 1962.[15] These decisions established that: (1) questions over the arbitrability of grievances are for an arbitrator and not the courts to decide; (2) in the absence of an express provision to exclude certain provisions from arbitration, all grievances arising under the contract must be subject to arbitration; and (3) the arbitrator's award must be enforced, even if his interpretation of the collective agreement differs from that of the court.

Thus, the Supreme Court has given arbitrators considerable latitude in their decision-making authority. The significance of this fact is of great consequence to the parties as they shape their arbitration machinery. In the process of negotiating their agreement, they must be very explicit in defining the areas of contract which are not subject to an arbitrator's review. Furthermore, the parties must be judicious in their selection of arbitrators.

Arbitrator Selection

Just as the parties were able to shape their grievance machinery through collective bargaining, they can also establish their arbitration machinery through bargaining. Thus, by the time an unresolved grievance reaches arbitration, the procedural arrangements to be followed for arbitrating the dispute have been outlined. To further our understanding of the process, however, we should note the various methods employed to resolve these procedural issues, particularly arbitrator selection.

Although the parties are free to select any arbitrator they mutually agree upon, there are several public or private organizations to assist them. Two such organizations, the Federal Mediation and Conciliation Service, a public agency of the federal government, and the American Arbitration Association, a private nonprofit organization, will supply the union and the management with a list of impartial arbitrators. Today, most agreements specify that the parties will select their arbitrator from a list of competent people supplied by one of these agencies. (See Table 2.) Using this list, the parties indicate their preference of arbitrators in accordance with some mutually acceptable formula. Additionally, a provision for breaking a possible deadlock is incorporated in most agreements. In such instances, the agreements provide for the submission of another list, or for final selection by the AAA or FMCS.

When the FMCS or the AAA is the participating outside agency, the parties are, in effect, agreeing to the use of a temporary ad hoc arbitrator. Selection on an ad hoc basis is the common procedure for small to medium sized companies. Given the relative infrequency of arbitrations in such companies, the parties are able to avoid the cost of retaining a permanent arbitrator. Thus, by maintaining a panel of competent, ad hoc arbitrators, the outside agencies perform a valuable service.

However, the agreement to use agency panels should not be regarded as a panacea. While there is an adequate number of untested arbitrators, there is a severe shortage of seasoned arbitrators, particularly on short notice. Since management and union representatives wish to obtain only the most experienced persons to hear their cases, they may be forced to delay selection until one is available. Such a delay may have an adverse effect upon an employee with an unresolved grievance, because the system had failed to perform its function, i.e., the rapid disposition of such grievances.

If the parties wish to avoid delay they may provide, as some agreements do, for the selection of a permanent arbitrator. This individual arbitrates each unresolved dispute. Therefore, in addition to the obvious advantage of availability, a permanent arbitrator system insures that the umpire will be a person with a firm understanding of the specific local plant and contract issue. In effect, the arbitrator can fashion a rule of law for the parties.

IMPORTANT NEW TERMS INTRODUCED

Grievance: An individual or group problem arising out of contract interpretation and application.

Grievance procedure: A method to administer and resolve individual and group problems during the life of the agreement.

Arbitration: A provision of the grievance procedure which requires submission of any unresolved grievances to a neutral third party.

SUGGESTED ADDITIONAL READINGS

Edwin F. Beal, Edward D. Wickersham, and Philip Kienast, *The Practice of Collective Bargaining,* 4th ed. (Homewood, Illinois: Richard D. Irwin, 1972) provides an excellent chapter on the various aspects of agreement administration.

Harold W. Davey, *Contemporary Collective Bargaining,* 3rd ed. (Englewood Cliffs: Prentice-Hall, 1972) provides a comprehensive treatment of grievance arbitration.

Paul Prasow and Edward Peters, *Arbitration and Collective Bargaining* (New York: McGraw Hill, 1970) provides a detailed summary of the legal basis of labor arbitration.

NOTES

[1] United States Department of Labor, *Major Collective Bargaining Agreements: Grievance Procedures,* Bulletin No. 1425-1, (Washington: U.S. Government Printing Office, 1964), p. 1.

[2] Ibid., p. 1.

[3] Robert Dubin, *The World of Work: Industrial Society and Human Relations,* (Englewood Cliffs: Prentice-Hall, 1958), p. 322.

[4] Supreme Court of the United States, *United Steelworkers of America v. Warrior Gulf Navigation Company,* June 20, 1960, 363 U.S. 574.

[5] *Agreement Between Paper Box Manufacturers and International Brotherhood of Pulp, Sulphite and Paper Mill Workers*—AFL-CIO.

[6] *Agreement Between Thorofare Markets, Inc., and the International Brotherhood of Teamsters, Chauffeurs, Warehousemen and Helpers of America*—IND.

[7] *Agreement Between H. K. Porter Company and International Brotherhood of Electrical Workers*—AFL-CIO.

[8] In a sense, the National War Labor Board imposed arbitration upon the parties. By order of the Board, arbitration provisions were written into collective agreements. The student should understand that such provisions were necessary to preclude the possibility of work stoppages in our key industries under conditions of war.

[9] United States Department of Labor, *Arbitration Provisions,* Bulletin No. 1425-6 (Washington: U.S. Government Printing Office, 1966), p. 5.

[10] Ibid., p. 1.

[11] Frequently, an arbitrator's decision will establish a precedent. Since arbitration is a quasi-judicial process, most arbitrators are reluctant to render subsequent decisions that are in variance with precedents. Obviously, then, the party which suffers most from an adverse arbitration decision should strive to have these stricken in the next contract negotiations.

[12] United States Department of Labor, *Arbitration Provisions,* p. 95.

[13] Labor-Management Relations Act, 1947, 80th Cong., 1st sess., C. 120, 61 Stat. 136, 29 U.S. C. 141-44, 171-88.

[14] *Textile Workers Union v. Lincoln Mills,* 353 U.S. 448 (1957).

[15] In each case, the *United Steelworkers of America* were the party requesting appeal. Brief summaries of each case may be found in the August 1960 publication of the *Monthly Labor Review.*

10

Public Employees: A New Horizon

INTRODUCTION

The organization of public employees in the U.S. is a recent development which holds considerable promise for the labor movement. Although the public sector has long been an area of significant employment growth, it has remained largely unorganized except for some public corporations, the naval shipyards, and the postal service. The absence of organization is explained in part by many positive prohibitions against union organization by public employees and in part by prohibitions and limitations on various union activities if unions did organize. For example, there existed a nearly universal prohibition of the right to strike by public employees. Potential union members and neutral observers often reasoned that inability of employees to strike meant, in effect, the inability of unions to exist. There was little benefit perceived by employees from a union that could not strike.

There exists both a history of and at least a pseudotheoretical support for these limitations. A brief explanation of each should aid in understanding the current situation. The history of our attitude toward public employee unions consists, in effect, of a single event, the Boston police strike of 1919. Members of the Boston police force had suffered what they considered very poor working conditions and inadequate wages for some time. A small, but vocal, minority of the force had organized and applied for an AFL charter in July 1919. The police administration suspended immediately all members of the organization. They announced that no policeman had the right to join a labor organization.

Approximately 75 percent of the policemen were on strike by September despite citizen attempts to mediate. The city was unprotected, and disorder prevailed. The mayor finally requested the state militia as a last resort. Samuel Gompers appealed to Massachusetts Governor Calvin Coolidge to assist in settlement of the strike, but he received only Coolidge's response that, "There is no right to strike against the public safety by anyone, anywhere, any time."[1] Coolidge called out the entire militia and supported the police commissioner's decision not to rehire any strikers. The strike was broken completely. This relatively brief episode became the foundation for our basic attitudes toward public employee unions and strikes.

The alternative contexts for viewing public employee strikes derived from this experience and continue to have a role in our public policy and treatment of public employee unions. The first is often referred to as the "sovereignty argument," and maintains that unions cannot strike the government because it is sovereign, i.e., a strike against government is equated to insurrection or an attempt to overthrow the government. It must be observed that if a government *is* sovereign power, then there is nothing to prevent it from permitting unions to organize, bargain collectively, and strike if it so wishes. Second, the observation must be made that equation of a strike with insurrection or an attempt to overthrow government probably falls somewhere between the peculiar and the absurd. For example, few persons viewing the strikes of garbage collectors in Memphis and hospital workers in Charleston, South Carolina, appeared to feel that the basic purposes of these actions was the overthrow of the governments of those cities, the respective states, or the U.S. Most persons appeared to view these actions as attempts to improve wages, hours, and working conditions, and nothing else. The point is that the argument equating public strikes and insurrection is a delusion designed to mask the issues.

The second alternative, which is simpler and more at the center of the issue, is the attempt to identify persons who perform essential services and to avoid interruption of essential services as much as possible. There is a recognition that persons who provide these services happen to work for government, but also that it is secondary whether they work for government or for a private employer. This distinction would prohibit strikes only by public employees who provide *essential* services. It seems the more rational of the two alternatives.

However, it is important in the pursuit of this alternative to avoid the identification as essential of those services whose interruption is really only an *inconvenience.* A strike by public school teachers, particularly in a large urban area, represents considerable inconvenience to the public and to parents of school children, but it is not an emergency.

Our experience with the so-called "national emergency strikes" under the Taft-Hartley Act provisions since 1948 has not been reassuring in this regard. Several studies have concluded that these provisions have been invoked too often in situations that represented inconveniences rather than emergencies. One respected opinion argues that:[2]

The fact that a strike in the basic steel industry could last fifty-five days in the midst of the Korean War without any of the dire consequences predicted by President Truman when he seized the industry, or by numerous commentators . . . is of main importance in any discussion of emergency dispute procedures.

Finally, we must note the present and the emerging significance of both government employment and union membership by government employees. There has been a marked increase in both statistics (Table 1). Even if government did not present special problems, its mere size and growth as an employer (and as a source of union membership) would require its inclusion in any study of labor relations.

TABLE 1
Government Employment and Union
Membership, Selected Dates, 1960-1970

Year	Government civilian employment	Union members	Membership as a percentage of employment
1960	7,935	1,070	13
1962	8,691	1,225	14
1964	9,350	1,453	16
1966	10,322	1,717	17
1968	11,590	3,857	33
1970	12,424	4,080	33

Source: *Manpower Report of the President* 1973, and *Directory of National Unions and Employee Associations (1971)*.

The authors turn now to a brief consideration of labor relations among federal and state government employees, particularly, in the latter category, among schoolteachers. Teacher unionism is selected for specific attention because it provides one focus for viewing the largely confused and complex situation in state labor relations and because it is an area of considerable public misunderstanding. We will include a discussion of the government as an employer, the structure of federal employee bargaining, and the "special case" of the teachers.

UNIQUE CHARACTER OF GOVERNMENT AS AN EMPLOYER

Much of the difficulty with and the legal restrictions on labor relations among public employees derives from some identifiable "peculiarities" of the government as an employer. We exclude the sovereignty argument because so few people really accept it. The specific peculiarities are (1) the nonprofit monopoly position of government, (2) the difficulty in defining who *is* the employer, (3) the general absence of methods for dispute resolution, (4) the limited amount of training materials, and (5) the political problem.[3]

The government's nonprofit monopoly status has many implications for collective bargaining. First, there are no "profits" in the usual sense to be divided between employer and employees. Governments are *labor intensive,* i.e., they employ much labor and not much of other productive resources. Therefore, wage increases are very much evident in government budgets to the eventual dismay of legislators and taxpayers. A given wage increase has more effect on the total budget than it would in less labor-intensive employments. This factor places a restraint on contract negotiations that is generally absent in the private sector.

The monopoly position of government balances this factor to some extent. In other words, there is often no other organization which can provide the goods and services that government supplies. This absence of "competition" may produce a lack of constraint on the negotiating parties in contrast to the private sector where the costs of settlements can affect the firm's market position via price increases. Finally, there is a strong public implication that government services will be provided without interruption—an implication or presumption confirmed by the existence of only two state laws which allow the right to strike by public employees. The current legal context conveys a clear conclusion that economic force, at least in the form of a work stoppage, is considered inappropriate.

The problem of defining who is, in fact, the employer is a major one for government labor relations. The problem has two components. The first concerns the definitions of appropriate bargaining units, employees, and management. The historical orientation of public employment suggests that all members of the organization—supervisors and supervised alike—are dedicated to provision of their public service. This aspect is particularly evident in the context of teacher unionism.

The second aspect is more complicated. Professor Davey has identified it in terms of a model of collective bargaining that includes two characters in addition to the usual employer-employee or union-management confrontation.[4] They are the elected representative body and the taxpayers. The problem may be that the union and management can resolve their disputes but that the resolution may not satisfy the other two characters.

There is no predefined or mutually accepted method for dispute resolution in many governmental labor relations settings. The method in the federal government is quite new; and less than one-half of the states have labor relations laws for public employment. The problem becomes one of neither party knowing what to do or where to go when an impasse occurs. There is an additional problem in the shortage of neutrals, mediators, and arbitrators even when a procedure is specified. This is one symptom of the more basic problem that virtually all of our labor relations experience has involved the private sector. Much of the experience in that sector cannot be transferred to public employee relations.

The final peculiarity involves "politics." For example, the postal unions "bargained" with the Post Office Department for many years through congressional lobbying activities. However, if real bargaining is to develop and to succeed, politics in this poorer sense of the word must be avoided. Professor Davey has stated the situation well:[5]

> ... If public bargaining is to become mature and stable, *there can be only one set of negotiations.* There should not be a second round with the legislative branch to achieve a fatter economic settlement ... the long-run consequences would be the certain breakdown of regularized bargaining ... Chaos would soon be the rule ...

The above analysis suggests that government represents a different type of employer in terms of labor relations. The authors consider now federal labor relations.

FEDERAL EMPLOYEE LABOR RELATIONS

A half century from now the student of labor relations who looks back may very well be forced to record in his memory the dates 1962 and 1970. These were the years of issuance of two Presidential Executive Orders which materially affected labor relations activities by federal employees. The Kennedy Executive Order (EO10988) represented the first occasion when federal employees in general were given positive encouragement in the process of organization and collective bargaining. The Nixon Order (EO11491) clarified in some very important structural ways EO10988 and served to reinforce the basic statement of policy.[6]

> Each employee of the Executive Branch of the Federal Government has the right, freely and without fear of penalty or reprisal, to form, join and assist a labor organization or to refrain from any such activity, and each employee shall be protected in the exercise of this right.

This policy covers all federal employees in the executive branch except those involved in work closely related to the national security. The major agency exceptions include the FBI, CIA, National Security Agency, Foreign Service, USIA, and AID.

The present structure, with a few significant exceptions, calls for the type of collective bargaining procedure which students of private employer collective bargaining have been conditioned to expect. There are provisions for determination of appropriate bargaining units, representative elections, exclusive representation,[7] and an identification of those subjects that represent items about which the parties are responsible for bargaining. The Executive Order identifies a typical "management rights" clause and requires that all contracts provide for a specified grievance procedure which *may* have as its terminal step arbitration. Labor unions seeking to represent federal employees must meet the same requirements as unions serviced by the National Labor Relations Board in terms of such things as internal union democracy, fiscal integrity and bonding requirements, union trusteeship, and nondiscrimination in membership requirements or treatment.

The present structure has three central administrative authorities: The Federal Labor Relations Council (FLRC), the Federal Service Impasse Panel (FSIP), and the Assistant Secretary for Labor-Management Relations (A/S). The composition and duties of each are summarized in Table 2.

It is particularly important to recognize that arbitration awards can be reversed or modified by FLRC only on the basis that arbitration awards for private employees can be reversed by Federal Court under Section 301 of the Taft-Hartley Act. The Executive Order also contains a group of six unfair labor practices each for both unions and federal agencies. Finally the policy directs the Department of Labor to collect and disseminate, on a continuing basis, information about organization and collective bargaining in the federal service. This activity, assuming that it is pursued on a reasonable basis, should prove to be of particular value to persons seeking to keep abreast of the working picture of federal labor relations.

Clearly EO11491 may not be the final answer to the many questions posed by unionization among federal employees. However at present it appears certain that it represents a movement in the right direction. Finally, it seems evident that the trend of increased unionization among federal employees and among public employees generally is the wave of the next decade.[8]

TEACHER UNIONISM

Although teachers are state and local employees, the authors will consider them as a separate group. First, strikes by teachers represent considerable inconvenience to the public. Second, unlike other public employees, the teacher has been cautioned that union membership would be "unprofessional." Until recently, teachers have tended to view this notion as a real barrier to joining a labor organization.[9] Third, teachers' salaries represent a slightly different problem than those of other public employees because their employers, the school districts, often have the authority to increase tax rates. Finally, teacher bargaining is an almost classic example of the difficulty in defining an "adversary" relationship between employer and employee that is common in collective bargaining. All persons in the school are charged with the

TABLE 2
Administrative Responsibility Federal Labor Relations — E011491

Federal Labor Relations Council (FLRC)	Federal Service Impasses Panel (FSIP)	Assistant Secretary of Labor for Labor-Management Relations (A/S)

1. Composition:
  a. Chairman: Civil Service Commission (CSC) Chairman
  b. Secretary of Labor
  c. Office of Management and Budget (OMB) Director
  d. Other Executive Branch officials at discretion of President
 	
2. Functions:
  a. Administer and interpret EO
  b. Decide major policy issues
  c. Report and make recommendations to President
 	
3. Discretion to consider:
  a. Appeals from Assistant Secretary of Labor for Labor-Management Relations (A/S) Decisions
  b. Appeals on negotiability issues
  c. Exceptions to arbitrators' awards
  d. Other appropriate matters
	Established as agency within FLRC to resolve negotiation impasses
	
	1. Composition: three or more members appointed by President (seven members appointed)
	
	2. Resolution procedures:
	  a. Disputes: Federal Mediation and Conciliation Service (FMCS) provides services and assistance to Federal agencies and labor organizations
	  b. Impasses: When voluntary arrangements, including resort to FMCS, fail, either party may request FSIP to take appropriate action
	
	3. Functions: Discretion to consider negotiation impasses and—
	  a. Recommend resolution procedures
	  b. Settle by appropriate action
	  c. Authorize or direct arbitration or third-party fact finding with recommendations
		1. Functions:
		  a. Decides cases involving questions of—
		    • Appropriate unit
		    • Unfair labor practice complaints
		    • Alleged violations of standards of conduct for labor organizations
		    • Whether grievances are subject to grievance or arbitration procedures in negotiated agreement
		    • Eligibility for National Consultation Rights under FLRC criteria
		  b. Supervises representation elections (mandatory for exclusive recognition) and certifies results
		  c. Issues cease and desist orders for unfair labor practice and standards of conduct violations, and/or requires appropriate affirmative action
		
		2. Appeals: Parties have right to appeal to FLRC, pursuant to its regulations, on major policy issues

Source: *Background and Major Provisions of Executive Order 11491, As Amended: Labor-Management Relations in the Federal Service* (Washington: U.S. Department of Labor, 1972), pp. 4-5.

concern for "good education," from the janitor to the school board member. The school superintendent has been viewed in this context not as a manager but as a "super teacher." This view was reinforced by the fact that many superintendents were, in fact, classroom teachers.

What continues to happen among teachers is that their dissatisfaction with low wages, poor working conditions, and little real control over what happens in the school finally overcomes the "sense of professionalism" and makes unionism an attractive alternative. Although teacher unionism is a very old phenomenon,[10] its emergence with any significance did not occur until the 1960s when increased teacher militancy combined with a revision of many state laws. For example, the organization of teachers in Michigan went from near zero to 80 percent in a five-year period of the 1960s. Membership of the American Federation of Teachers increased nationally from 50,000 in 1956 to 205,320 in 1970.[11]

Teacher collective bargaining is a reality in many states today and the horizon of tomorrow in the others, but several problems remain. First, it is obvious that regardless of the law there will be teachers' strikes when negotiations or grievance handling break down. However, one must note that schools often close for other reasons, such as athletic victories, harvests, national holidays, teacher meetings, etc., without any apparent damage to the educational process.

The second problem, particularly in the absence of a well-defined law, concerns the appropriate scope of teacher bargaining. It is likely that questions of school curriculum, room sizes, scheduling, and educational goals will be excluded from bargaining. In any case, the scope question is likely to be a lively issue for some time.

The third problem concerns interunion competition. There continues to be a rivalry between the American Federation of Teachers, AFL-CIO (AFT) and the National Education Association (NEA). Historically the NEA has emerged stronger in numbers of members when there were confrontations. It stressed "professional behavior" and used "professional negotiation" to describe collective bargaining and "sanctions" to describe strikes. The competition appears to have strengthened both organizations and to have narrowed the substantive differences in their approaches.

The fourth problem involves the impact of organization and bargaining on the structure of school districts. Some smaller (and more costly to operate) districts may be forced to merge in order to have sufficient staff to deal with the new labor relations issues. Increased wages for teachers may compel merger in order to increase the tax base.

CONCLUSIONS

We have reviewed the history of public employee unionism and have explored the contemporary scene that is emerging. The nature of this chapter reflects the nature of public employee unionism—tentative and changing rapidly but clearly established. It may be that public employee unionism will rival "blue-collar" unionism as the important form of U.S. labor-management relations in the future. The question occupying students in the next several years may likely be the extent to which our private sector experience of the past 40 years is relevant or transferable to the public sector.

IMPORTANT NEW TERMS INTRODUCED

Sovereignty concept: The notion that organized government can be viewed only within the context of representing a supreme political authority which cannot be legally attached.

Kennedy and Nixon Executive Orders: Two separate Presidential Executive Orders which form the present operating framework of labor-management relations for federal employees.

Public employee unionism: Term used to describe the unique organizing, bargaining, and other forms of economic action pursued on behalf of employees of the federal, state, and local governments.

SUGGESTED ADDITIONAL READINGS

Albert A. Blum (ed.), *Teacher Unions and Associations: A Comparative Study* (Urbana: University of Illinois Press, 1967).

E. D. Duryea, et al., *Faculty Unions and Collective Bargaining* (San Francisco: Jossey-Bass, 1973).

Jack Stieber, *Public Employee Unionism: Structure, Growth, Policy* (Washington: The Brookings Institution, 1973).

Robert T. Woodworth and Richard B. Peterson, *Collective Negotiation for Public and Professional Employees* (Glenview: Scott, Foresman, 1969).

NOTES

[1] See William Allen White, *A Puritan in Babylon: The Story of Calvin Coolidge* (New York: Macmillan, 1938), p. 166.

[2] Herbert R. Northrup and Gordon F. Bloom, *Government and Labor: The Role of Government in Union-Management Relations* (Homewood: Richard D. Irwin, 1963), p. 368.

[3] This listing is not exhaustive. A more detailed analysis is contained in Harold W. Davey, *Contemporary Collective Bargaining,* 3rd edition (Englewood Cliffs: Prentice-Hall, 1972), pp. 334-360.

[4] Ibid., pp. 346-347.

[5] Ibid., p. 353.

[6] *Background and Major Provisions of Executive Order 11491, As Amended: Labor-Management Relations in the Federal Service* (Washington: U.S. Department of Labor, 1972), p. 3.

[7] An exception to this concept is a status called "national consultation rights,"

for unions, not the bargaining agent but with "substantial membership" and only when there is no agent.

[8] For example, see Abraham L. Gitlow, "The Trade Union Prospect in the Coming Decade," *Labor Law Journal,* XXI (March 1970), pp. 131-158.

[9] A full discussion of this notion is contained in Harold W. Davey, "Professional Security Is Your Professional Right," *The Bulletin* (Official journal of the Iowa Nurses' Association), Spring 1965.

[10] The first teacher union in New York City dates from 1916. See Stephen Cole, *The Unionization of Teachers: A Case Study of the UFT* (New York: Praeger, 1969).

[11] *Directory of National Unions and Employee Associations* 1971 (Washington: U.S. Department of Labor, 1972), p. 113; and *Directory of National and International Unions in the United States, 1969* (Washington: U.S. Department of Labor, 1970), p. 93.

11

The Future of Collective Bargaining

INTRODUCTION

Future students of labor may review the early part of the decade of the 1970s and refer to it as the period when persons became concerned seriously about the future content and structure of collective bargaining. There have been and continue to be numerous conferences of both academics and practitioners centered on the theme of "the future of collective bargaining." Speaking to the 1971 Collective Bargaining Forum, then Secretary of Labor (and former industrial relations director of a major aerospace firm) James D. Hodgson observed:[1]

> ... I see the need for a real defense of collective bargaining. And to defend it we need to refine it, improve it, and adapt it to the changing needs of our times ... we should examine its deficiencies and try selectively to correct them.

> What are these deficiencies? Where is collective bargaining failing us? It is easy to develop a list.

> ... Certainly collective bargaining is failing us in dealing with emergency disputes in the transportation industry, particularly the railroads ...

> Collective bargaining is also failing in the construction industry, where a

basic problem seems to center around the multiplicity of fragmented bargaining units.

It is failing on the nation's farms simply because we have not used it there . . .

It may be too early to tell if it is failing in the rapidly growing public sector of our economy. But it is *not* too early to say that if it is to succeed there, we need new approaches—approaches that may be quite different from those we use in the private sector . . .

How can we correct these deficiencies? Some of them will require new laws . . . But more than new laws are needed . . .

We are consumed with matters of processes and tactics. We tend to forget the external effects—effects on the public and on the nation . . .

Finally, there is that old bugaboo—resistance to change . . . among traditionalists on both sides there is a tendency to cling to established public positions after the stream of history has passed them by . . .

A well-known industrial relations executive, Douglas Soutar, provided the following observations on the future of collective bargaining a year after Mr. Hodgson's remarks:[2]

While the extent of unionization has progressed little during the last 25 years in terms of percentage of total working population . . . the power of labor unions has increased dramatically . . . Employers, unable to resist this power at the bargaining table, have found their ability to manage effectively severely limited . . .

. . . it seems probable that if our system of economics is to survive until 1998 . . . there must be some swinging back of the pendulum to reduce union power . . .

. . . The present drift towards co-determination . . . will see progress by 1998, provided unions are willing to shoulder more of the burdens of responsibility than they have evidenced thus far . . .

Public employees will be almost totally organized by 1998 as will most service employees . . .

Many aspects of collective bargaining will be mechanical through computer systems by 1998 . . .

Union political and legislative activity . . . will intensify . . .

Wages . . . will of necessity be limited by those in other countries, and, in the case of the more highly-industrialized nations, will almost approximate our own.

. . . job security requirements will tend to divert wages into benefits, such as improved pensions . . .

. . . Continued abuses of workmen's compensation systems will produce more rigid administration and legislation (under a federal system) . . .

Hospital-medical-surgical benefits will largely exist under a federal system much like social security . . .

These two experts and many others who have spoken or written on the subjects[3] have identified broadly three areas in which collective bargaining and the environment in which it occurs are likely to change in the future: (1) the labor market, (2) the "structure" of collective bargaining, and (3) the legal setting for collective bargaining. We have explored the first of these areas in detail in Chapter 2. Therefore, we devote our attention to the latter two areas in this chapter. We look first at the current trends in collective bargaining and then at the legal environment.

CURRENT TRENDS

From among the many and complex trends in collective bargaining that are likely to continue and to be magnified in the future, several of the more important ones are considered here—the growth in importance of public employee unions, the role of the strike in collective bargaining, and coalition bargaining.

Public Employee Unions

One of the significant characteristics of the labor movement during the past decade or two is the diminution in, or at times absence of, the rate of growth in union membership. Union membership, as a percentage of the civilian nonagricultural labor force, is no larger today than it was some 20 years ago. The explanations for this phenomenon, ranging from the decreased numbers of "blue-collar" workers who were traditionally the major component of union membership to the inability of unions to organize southern workers, have been explored in previous chapters. The notion that organization of white-collar workers in the private sector would offset membership losses among blue-collar workers has proven false with the repeated failures of union organizing campaigns among these workers.

However, the experience with both "white-" and "blue-collar" workers in the public sector has been the opposite during recent years. Public employees, from trash collectors to college professors, have demonstrated at an increasing rate their desire for collective bargaining and union membership. The magnitude of this desire was detailed in Chapters 6 and 10. But what of the future?

It is obvious first that many public employees will form unions, attempt to negotiate, and (if unsuccessful in either recognition or negotiation) engage in work stoppages, *whether or not* there is legislation that permits or prohibits such activities by public employees. The attitudes of some public officials and legislators that public employee organization and negotiation can be prevented if there is no enabling legislation or if there is prohibitive legislation have been proved incorrect. Therefore, all states will have to adopt legislation that provides an orderly procedure for handling the issues of recognition, negotiation, and contract administration. Failure to enact such legislation will merely create a vacuum within which the forces of economic and political power are likely to replace those of order and reason to the detriment of the workers, the government, and the public.

A second and related issue concerns work stoppages by public employees and the need for provision of alternatives to such stoppages. The authors distinguished in Chapter 10 various groups of public employees based on the potential harm that might result from their engaging in work stoppages. However, it remains unlikely that the general public or their elected representatives will accept work stoppages by public employees in the same manner that strikes by private sector workers are tolerated. Therefore, alternatives must be developed to settle unresolved contract negotiation disputes.

Several alternatives to work stoppages are possible. *Fact-finding* involves the employment of a third party neutral to investigate the dispute and to make recommendations for a settlement to the parties and perhaps to the public.[4] This process may be effective when coupled to strong public sentiment. However, it does not usually include any means for enforcement beyond moral suasion. *Compulsory arbitration* involves the employment of a third-party neutral to decide the terms of the settlement.[5] This procedure produces a settlement that may be enforced in the courts. However, it is limited by several factors. Should the government be permitted to abdicate its role as public manager to a third party? Can a third party establish contract terms that might require imposition of additional taxes to finance them? Various other proposals for *quasi-strikes* or procedures which impose the traditional burdens (i.e., loss of wages and loss of revenues) on each party to a work stoppage but which allow continuation of the services have also been suggested.[6] These proposals are the most intriguing of the alternatives suggested. They suffer the weakness in some cases of an absence of something approximating profits. For example, workers in the private sector might agree to continue working but to receive only part of their wages; the employer would agree as well to donate part of his profits to charity, etc. The result is a situation which approximates the penalties of a strike but without a cessation of work. The problem in the public sector is the absence in many situations of "profit."

It seems likely that most states will ultimately adopt legislation to permit strikes by what were referred to in Chapter 10 as employees providing nonessential public services. As stated above, many such employees will strike with or without a law. They will do so in the knowledge that public officials can, for example, send striking trash collectors to jail but will remain unable to get the trash collected. It is likely that many states will adopt fact-finding or compulsory arbitration legislation for those employees providing essential services.[7]

The Role of the Strike

The logic of a strike in the private sector is that it imposes costs on each party. Workers lose wages; employers lose profits. As the duration of the strike lengthens, the parties will be compelled to reach a compromise solution to their differences because the costs will become too high. In fact, the strike does not seem to be fulfilling this role in many instances. Apart from the inconvenience to the general public and any threat to national health and safety, other limitations are recognized. Workers in some states can collect unemployment insurance and public welfare benefits in addition to union-financed strike relief payments. Many others will find alternative employment during the strike. As automated technology is introduced, many employers find it possible to continue production without the striking employees by using management personnel. In fact, the absence of the striking workers may provide a convenient time to install labor-saving equipment that ultimately replaces the workers. For these and other reasons, a strike once set into motion may not produce pressures for a settlement but instead produce a greater unwillingness to compromise.

These considerations and those of public inconvenience have led to experiments (largely unsuccessful) with alternatives to the strike. These have included those mentioned above in connection with public employees. An additional alternative is one called variously *continuous bargaining* or *joint consultation*. The best-publicized example has occurred in the steel industry, but the general procedures are similar in all industries.[8] Briefly, the management and union representatives attempt to avoid the "crisis" bargaining that results from compression of the bargaining process into a short time period that recurs with each impending expiration of the agreement. Instead the parties meet and confer throughout the duration of the agreement in an effort to resolve as many issues as possible before the beginning of formal contract negotiations. The logic of this approach is that most issues will be solved prior to negotiations, thus allowing all parties to be familiar in advance with the issues and to concentrate their efforts on the few remaining unresolved issues.

It is unlikely that there will be widespread adoption of these procedures in a formal manner. However, it seems probable that such procedures will simply evolve as the parties and the public become less enchanted with the use of the strike weapon. This evolution may be promoted by the threat of governmental intervention as a strike alternative.

Coalition Bargaining

The concept of "coordinated bargaining" or "coalition bargaining" was introduced in Chapter 8. The concept derives from situations in which more than one union represents the employees of a given firm, in which a firm has several plants whose various employees are represented by different unions, or in which the "parent" company of a conglomerate corporation controls several companies each of which has employees represented by different unions. If the unions negotiate separately, their bargaining positions are weakened. For example, one union may find a strike at one firm or plant to be ineffective because the employer transfers production to another plant that is operating because its employees work under a different agreement which is still in effect. The unions obtain several important benefits from coordinated bargaining, or from bargaining together with all firms of the conglomerate or with all plants of the firm. They are aware of the issues in all negotiations and of the arguments made. They can prevent the firm from negotiating an agreement with the weakest union first and then using it as a "model" for the others. They can make a strike more effective by eliminating the possibility of the firm's maintaining production at other plants.

It is likely that the trend to coordinated bargaining will intensify. More firms are being absorbed into a conglomerate structure. The costs of strikes to unions and their members are increasing, thus increasing the desire to have fewer small strikes involving components of the same firm. Finally, the gains from coordinated bargaining to the unions, particularly in the electrical industry, have been significant.[9]

GOVERNMENT INTERVENTION

It is clear that the future of collective bargaining depends to a substantial extent upon future shifts in the role of government. The remainder of this chapter is devoted to that subject. Although what follows is divided into two major topics—government intervention and reform of labor law—it is important to remember that this division is largely artificial and one of convenience. Also it is important to remember that considerations of government and of labor law reform are closely related. Often one implies or perhaps requires the other.

National Emergency Strikes

National emergency strikes represent an area in which direct government intervention has a long history. The federal government, beginning with several railroad strikes in the 1870s, has evidenced considerable willingness to intervene in situations which someone felt represented emergencies. The Pullman Strike reviewed earlier represented a similar activity. In both world wars, special machinery was established to enable government intervention in situations in which a threat to national security might be created by a work stoppage. The Railway Labor Act, passed during the interwar period, provides a specific mechanism for handling disputes which appear to be potentially emergency situations. The Taft-Hartley Act, passed during the post-World War II strike wave, contains provisions for coping with strikes thought to represent national emergencies. There are many other examples.

Definition of an Emergency

There have been many attempts to define national emergency situations in an adequate manner. Some of these attempts have been very ad hoc, i.e., President Cleveland in the Pullman Strike, President Truman in the 1949 Steel Strike, and Governor Calvin Coolidge in the Boston Police Strike. Others, such as the Railway Labor and Taft-Hartley Acts, have been in the form of specific legislation. Several respected students of labor relations have indicated either that there seems little reason to believe that there *are* national emergency strikes[10] or that our present procedures are simply not very satisfactory for dealing with whatever it is that they attempt to deal with.[11] By contrast, much literature exists which actively attempts to define, before the fact of any active dispute, what type of situation would have to be present for the existence of a national emergency. Professor George Hildebrand devoted substantial effort to this task and eventually[12] evolved an operational definition of a national emergency using the following criteria: (1) national rather than local impact, (2) essential products, (3) all or a very substantial proportion of the industry, and (4) actual rather than speculative. He identified five industries in which strikes could conceivably lead to national emergencies. Unfortunately, later research has concluded that in most (if not all) of these industries, output lost because of a strike seems to be replaced or "made up" in a relatively short period of time because of the industries' typical production patterns which are well below either maximum or optimal levels.[13] Therefore, it is not clear that national emergency strikes exist. On the other hand, it is clear that the public *believes,* that they do, in fact, exist and (perhaps more important to public policy) feels strongly that something needs to be done about such strikes. It is equally clear that neither the appointment of special Presidential Boards (under the Railway Labor Act) nor the 80-day injunction procedure (under the Taft-Hartley Act) represents a solution that has worked.[14]

Alternatives to the Present Approach

One way to realize the difficulty of coping effectively with the problem of emergency strikes is to catalog the suggested alternatives. Some observers have suggested the seemingly simple alternative of *compulsory arbitration* (see above). Any bargaining impasse identified by the appropriate public official would have to be submitted to a third party for binding arbitration. Apart from the mechanical objections to this alternative (e.g., selection of the arbitrator), the major weakness seems to be the projected potential effect on the bargaining process. Experience under one state law[15] and with congressional handling of the 1963 and 1967 railroad strikes indicates that the net effect of a compulsory arbitration provision seems to be reduction of the parties' willingness to engage in the traditional "give and take" of bargaining, apparently from fear of weakening a potential arbitration case. Although our experience with compulsory arbitration is quite limited, its prospects as a successful alternative appear to be even more limited.

One of the more inventive alternatives is generally called either the "nonstrike strike" or the "statutory" strike mentioned above.[16] The major difficulty is finding agreement on the amount of "penalty" that each party must suffer, how penalties are to be collected, and what will be their eventual disposition. Each of these questions represents more than a simple procedural disagreement. The answer to each can affect significantly the bargaining position, power, and relations of the parties. Despite the apparently great attraction of the statutory strike for emergency situations, the obvious problems are substantial.

Another alternative would combine a series of specific alternatives into what has become known as a "choice of procedures" concept. This approach, which was contained in a 1947 Massachusetts law covering public utility disputes, provides some governmental official (perhaps a governor) with some choices (in Massachusetts, mediation, voluntary arbitration, government seizure, or forced extension of the agreement for a specified period of time) to invoke in cases involving strikes in essential industries. Again this notion has substantial theoretical appeal. However, there are two major objections in practice. First, substantial and, in some cases, compelling shortcomings exist in some of the components normally included among the choices. For example, compulsory arbitration retains the same weaknesses as it possessed alone. Perhaps more compelling is the objection that the emphasis of the parties may shift easily from collective bargaining to bargaining with the governmental authority which must evolve the procedure.[17]

The most recent proposal is one advanced by President Nixon in 1970, which consisted of three elements. These were (1) extension of the Taft-Hartley "cooling-off" period if a settlement appeared near, (2) requirement that at least part of an affected industry remain operative, and (3) a complicated and thinly veiled form of eventual compulsory arbitration. Both union and management spokesmen reacted to the proposal with predictable great disfavor.

This brief review of some major alternative proposals has hopefully served to increase the student's perception of the national emergency disputes problem. The questions that emerge are (1) whether there are "national emergency strikes" in peacetime, (2) whether there exists a satisfactory solution, and (3) whether it is possible that our problem as a society is the unwillingness to accept the inconvenience required occasionally by our professed belief in free collective bargaining. These issues are important to the future of collective bargaining if only because we seem to come back to them continually.

Wage Controls

Public concern with the relationship between inflation and collective bargaining in its current form began in 1962 with promulgation of the "wage-price guidelines" by the President's Council of Economic Advisors (CEA). They formalized, in a sense, the informal techniques of persuasion used by many presidents to exercise moderation in bargaining settlements. The CEA guidelines attempted to limit percentage wage increases to the average percentage increases in productivity on the assumption that wages could not then cause inflation. Collective bargaining would be allowed to function within guidelines established for the general benefits of society.

At best, the experience with the guidelines between 1962 and 1966 can be described as moderately successful. Union and management officials argued that their representatives should have been involved in establishment of the guidelines. Like any average, the guideline figure was unfair to some segments of a society as varied as ours. There was some inconsistency in application of the guidelines. Organized labor objected to the absence of any limitations on profits. These complaints proved ultimately persuasive and formal restraints ended in 1966. It should be noted in passing that the Consumer Price Index increased by 7 percent during the five years of guidelines compared to 11 percent during the preceding five years and 21 percent for the five years after the guidelines.[18]

Nixon's "New Economic Policy"

As a result of continuing inflation, President Nixon exercised in 1971 his authority under the Economic Stabilization Act of 1970 and established a series of Boards to monitor bargaining settlements in the construction industry. Six months later, he established the first of four phases of a program to control domestic wages and prices. Phase I was an absolute freeze on wages, prices, interest, and rent but not (to the unions' great dissatisfaction) prices. It was predictably successful. Phase II included substantial controls over wages and prices, the former administered by a tripartite Pay Board. Phase III marked a return to voluntary restraints. Beginning in August 1973, there was in Phase IV a return to more specific controls, particularly over wages, but the controls were limited and short-lived. The notion of controlling wages, particularly those resulting from major bargaining settlements, was consistent throughout the four phases.

The increased inflation resulting from the "oil crisis" that began in 1973 placed organized labor and the national government in difficult positions. The public reacted unfavorably to any attempt by the unions to achieve large wage increases. However, the unions faced increased pressure from their members to achieve wage settlements that would enable them to "catch up" with inflation.

Appeals from the national administrations to the unions through formal or informal means to limit wage increases to avoid inflation are, in some senses, unfair. The recognition of three obvious facts by the administrations is needed. (1) The unions are caught between the conflicting forces of public opinion and membership demands. (2) Both inflation and the energy crisis exacted significant reductions in workers' real incomes. (3) The administration must extend some "trade-off" to the workers if it expects restraint in wage settlements. Failure to recognize these issues could force unions to build inflationary clauses into their agreements.

We have observed in this brief review that government intervention in the collective bargaining process can succeed if such intervention proceeds with the tacit consent of the governed and with a realistic view of the nature of the problem faced. One hopes that future governments learn from history.

REFORM OF LABOR LAW

Few subjects in our society represent more hearty perennials than "reform" of labor legislation. For the purposes of this chapter, our discussion is limited to proposed reforms or amendments of legislation regulating collective bargaining. This section includes two major areas of current concern—antitrust coverage of unions and the operation of the National Labor Relations Board (NLRB).

Antitrust Coverage

The evolution of antitrust coverage of unions was traced in Chapter 7. As indicated there, the Supreme Court adopted a position in the mid-1940s which seemed to be general, definitive, and permanent, i.e., that unions could pursue *any* legitimate union goal without fear of Sherman Act prosecution as long as they did not cooperate with nonlabor groups. This freedom of action was reduced by limitations in the Taft-Hartley and Landrum-Griffin Acts, such as limitations on secondary boycotts and jurisdictional disputes, but the unions remained generally free to pursue normal goals with most of the weapons at their disposal.

The Supreme Court apparently had cause to reconsider at least one aspect of antitrust coverage in 1965. In what was heralded as a landmark decision, *United Mine Workers v. Pennington*,[19] the Court held effectively that a union was responsible, under the Sherman Act, when it attempted to impose a uniform industry wage settlement after concluding negotiations with one group of employers. The results of this decision became more significant for the unions when the Court upheld a decision awarding $1.5 million in a treble-damage suit against the Mine Workers. Although there have been relatively few court actions like the *Pennington* case, the shift in judicial attitude that it reflects is a potentially threatening one for the labor movement because few, if any, strikes fail to interrupt the flow of commerce.

Proposed Legislative Changes

There has been no shortage of proposed legislation on the antitrust coverage of unions in recent years. Three of these proposals have been selected for comment. Few people seriously suggest blanket coverage of unions by the antitrust laws.[20] If unions are to exist and pursue effectively their reason for being, they must enjoy some of the characteristics associated normally with monopolies. The question that most legislative reform proposals consider is the degree to which unions should be limited in the exercise of that monopoly power. One suggestion proposes elimination of all situations in which unions bargain on a multiemployer basis. Another would limit any cooperation among local unions. Finally, some proposals would limit the operations of an international union to a single industry.

Many industrial relations observers feel that most, if not all, of these proposals are oriented in the wrong direction, i.e., they look back. Most academic opinion argues that what is needed is not a reversion to the late nineteenth century but rather the exercise of both reality and inventiveness. Reality involves the simple fact that unions must apparently be monopolies to some large degree in order to function adequately. Inventiveness is needed to cope with those aspects of union behavior which need to be restrained and can be restrained presumably without placing the entire institution under antitrust restrictions.

Reform of the NLRB

As noted earlier, the NLRB handles two types of case, those involving representation elections and those involving unfair labor practices. By specific legislative directive, the NLRB processes initially all representation cases through its regional offices which are located in major industrial cities. Although NLRB decisions may be appealed, the majority are settled in the regional offices. An average representation case requires 49 days for settlement.

By contrast, unfair labor practice cases cannot be resolved regionally but must be considered by at least three members of the Board. The average unfair labor practice case requires over 300 days for settlement. This figure does not include time involved in cases appealed to the courts.

The difference in time required to process the two types of case goes beyond inconvenience. Unfair labor practice cases by nature occur frequently in situations in which time is very important. Many occur during organizing campaigns. Substantial delay in those situations can result in the resolution of the problem occurring when it is no longer significant. One union active in the South has argued that some employers knowingly commit unfair labor practices designed to impede organizing because they recognize that the timeliness of the organizing campaign will have passed by the time the Board resolves the case.

Two alternatives have been proposed. One would make NLRB orders, which presently lack legal status,[21] self-enforcing, i.e., although still subject to court appeal, the orders would carry an automatic contempt-of-court quality if disobeyed during the interim. The other proposal would place all unfair labor practice actions in the federal courts.[22] The advocates argue that, among other things, recourse to the federal district courts would shorten the time lag involved in the present system. In addition to decreased time in handling the cases, proponents content that movement to the courts would promote greater stability and consistency in decisions. Opponents contend that federal court dockets are already overcrowded, and that district judges have rendered widely differing opinions in labor cases. Some proponents go even further and advocate a labor court system to replace the NLRB altogether.

SUGGESTED ADDITIONAL READINGS

Derek C. Bok and John T. Dunlop, *Labor and the American Community* (New York: Simon and Schuster, 1970).

NOTES

[1] J. D. Hodgson, "Challenges to Collective Bargaining," in Gerald W. Cormick (ed.), *Collective Bargaining Today: Proceedings of the Collective Bargaining Forum–1971* (Washington: The Bureau of National Affairs, 1972), pp. 81-87.

[2] Douglas Soutar, "A Forward Look at Labor-Management Relations Within the Framework of a Free Enterprise System," Gerald G. Somers (ed.), *The Next Twenty-five Years of Industrial Relations* (Madison: Industrial Relations Research Association, 1973), pp. 147-164.

[3] For example, see Richard L. Rowan (ed.), *Collective Bargaining: Survival in the 70's,* Report No. 5, Proceedings of a Conference Sponsored by the Industrial Research Unit and the Labor Relations Council, Wharton School, University of Pennsylvania (Philadelphia: University of Pennsylvania, 1972).

[4] For example, see Barbara Doering, "Impasse Issues in Teacher Disputes Submitted to Fact Finding in New York," *The Arbitration Journal,* 27, No. 1 (March 1972), pp. 1-17.

[5] Howard G. Foster, "Final Offer Selection in National Emergency Disputes," *The Arbitration Journal,* 27, No. 2 (June 1972), pp. 85-97, contains information on one of the newer proposals in this area.

[6] For example, see Michael L. Brookshire and J. Fred Holly, "Resolving Bargaining Impasses Through Gradual Pressure Strikes," *Labor Law Journal,* 24, No. 10 (October 1973), pp. 662-670.

[7] See Anthony V. Sinicropi and Thomas P. Gilroy, "The Legal Framework of Public Sector Dispute Resolution," *The Arbitration Journal,* 28, No. 1 (March 1973), pp. 1-13.

[8] See James J. Healy (ed.), *Creative Collective Bargaining: Meeting Today's Challenges to Labor-Management Relations* (Englewood Cliffs: Prentice-Hall, 1965) for descriptions of the early efforts in this direction.

[9] See William L. Chernish, *Coalition Bargaining: A Study of Union Tactics and Public Policy* (Philadelphia: University of Pennsylvania, 1969).

[10] Cyrus S. Ching, *Review and Reflections* (New York: B. C. Forbes, 1953), p. 103.

[11] Donald E. Cullen, "The Taft-Hartley Act in National Emergency Disputes," *Industrial and Labor Relations Review,* 6, No. 2 (October 1953), pp. 22-35; and———, *National Emergency Strikes* (Ithaca: New York State School of Industrial and Labor Relations, 1968).

[12] George H. Hildebrand, "An Economic Definition of the National Emergency Dispute," Irving Bernstein et al. (eds.), *Emergency Disputes and National Policy* (New York: Harper, 1955), pp. 6-15.

[13] C. L. Christenson, "Theory of the Offset Factor," *American Economic Review,* 43, No. 4 (September 1953), pp. 513-547; and *Collective Bargaining in the Basic Steel Industry* (Washington; U.S. Government Printing Office, 1961), pp. 3-18.

[14] John T. Dunlop, "The Settlement of Emergency Disputes," *Proceedings of the Fifth Annual Meeting* (Madison: Industrial Relations Research Association, 1952), pp. 112-133; *National Emergency Disputes Under the Labor-Management Relations Act, 1947-65* (Washington: U.S. Government Printing Office, 1966); Charles M. Rehmus, "Operation of the National Emergency Provisions of LMRA," *Yale Law Journal* 62 (1953), pp. 1042-1059; and J. Alexander, "Presidential Interventionism: The Crisis in Collective Bargaining," *Mississippi Valley Journal of Business and Economics,* 3, No. 3 (Spring, 1967), pp. 23-27.

[15] "Governor's Committee Report on New Jersey Public Utility Labor Disputes Act," *Industrial and Labor Relations Review,* 8, No. 3 (April 1955), pp. 403-427.

[16] One of the better articles on this subject is Leroy Marceau and Richard A. Musgrave, "Strikes in Essential Industries: A Way Out," *Harvard Business Review* (May 1949), p. 287 ff.

[17] See A. H. Raskin, "Collective Bargaining and the Public Interest," Lloyd Ulman (ed.), *Challenges to Collective Bargaining* (Englewood Cliffs: Prentice-Hall, 1967), pp. 155-168, for an excellent discussion of this topic.

[18] *Manpower Report of the President—March 1973* (Washington: U.S. Government Printing Office, 1973), p. 244.

[19] U.S. Supreme Court, *June 7, 1965.*

[20] Henry C. Simons, *Economic Policy for a Free Society* (Chicago: University of Chicago Press, 1948), Chapter 6, contains an analysis of the position of those who favor total antitrust coverage of unions.

[21] NLRB cease-and-desist orders can now be enforced by federal district courts, but the procedure is not automatic because one of the parties or the NLRB must seek enforcement.

[22] A thorough review of these proposals is contained in Guy Farmer, *Collective Bargaining in Transition: Restoring the Balance* (New York: Industrial Relations Counselors, 1967) and in Fritz L. Lyne, "The National Labor Relations Board and Suggested Alternatives," *Labor Law Journal,* 22, No. 7 (July 1971), pp. 408-423.

12

Personnel Management

The purpose of this chapter is to introduce the various schools of management thought and the impact each has had on the individual in the business enterprise. Particular emphasis is placed on the individual because the effective organization of human effort has always been one of the most pressing problems facing both past and contemporary management. This problem is the common element of each school of thought, regardless of the point in time in which the school developed. Each differs, however, in its approach. Through an understanding of this panorama of approaches, the student should be better equipped to understand contemporary management. Each of the diverse approaches has had its influence on modern management thinking.

The student should not consider the authors' treatment of the various approaches as exhaustive descriptions. The treatments are necessarily brief. As in other chapters, however, sources for more detailed readings are provided in the form of footnotes and suggested readings.

THE IMPETUS FROM THE INDUSTRIAL REVOLUTION

The industrial revolution which occurred in England during the middle of the eighteenth century provided the greatest impetus to the development of management thought. Prior to this time no systematic studies of management had been attempted because it was not necessary. Such industrial activity as did exist was accomplished through hand craftsmanship. In these small shop settings, masters and owners were in continuous close contact with the people working for them. The work situation was family-centered and any work problems that did exist were resolved on a personal level among friends.

The industrial revolution, however, drastically altered this work environment. Work in the emerging factory system required a new discipline. In contrast to variety and irregularity that once characterized the family-centered work environment, the workday and work functions became standardized.[1] Promptness, diligence, and production quotas became new words in the lexicon of every factory manager. The purpose was, of course, to make the worker compatible to machine production.

The lot of the worker deteriorated. Often he was treated as a pure factor of production, much the same as a machine. Compounding the worker's plight was a philosophical ethic which stressed individualism and placed the responsibility for his plight on his own idleness. Economists like John Stuart Mill argued that the only way to improve the lot of the working class was through education because education would make him more responsible.[2] Within this social environment, the voices of industrial critics were all too often silenced and excessively poor treatment of the worker continued through the eighteenth and most of the nineteenth century.

By the end of the nineteenth century, however, the efforts of industrial critics were beginning to have some effect. This was particularly true in the United States where the industrial revolution occurred many years later than it did in England. As the century drew to a close in the United States, the settlement of the frontier lands in the West was almost complete; the era of the "rugged individual" was over. He no longer had a choice between working in a factory or settling new lands. The individual and American society were becoming increasingly dependent upon industrial employment and production. In this new social environment of dependence and cooperation, the philosophy of "rugged individualism" became less relevant. Thus, while the effects of industrialization were felt much later in America than in England, the effects on the worker were only slightly less severe. The American worker did not suffer as long because he was able to draw upon the experiences of his English counterparts. He also benefited from the support of industrial critics who had earlier attacked the excesses of industrialization in England.

While the American socioeconomic environment was changing, a change was also taking place within the laboring class. Workers and their leaders began to devise a strategy for coping with this new socioeconomic environment. If their station in life was their own responsibility, then they would make a unified effort to correct it. The workers joined with earlier industrial critics and formed labor unions and labor parties. Through solidarity, they sought to end the excesses they had suffered. These collective efforts were instrumental in curbing business excesses in the area of health and safety, wages, and the length of the workday. Labor was no longer to be treated as a mere tool of production.

Concomitant to the sweeping changes in the labor sector and socioeconomic environment were changes in the form and mode of management. The master craftsmen had already been supplanted by the industrial entrepreneurs who found themselves at the helm of industries whose growth had been more explosive than gradual or sequential. They were charged with the responsibility of guiding increasingly complex enterprises. In a word, they needed assistance. To satisy this need, they created a new and special type of labor—the "hired manager." Similar to the labor he was to manage, the "hired manager" had no inherent right to ownership of the tools of production. His job, continuance in that job, and promotion would depend upon how well he accomplished his assigned task, namely, profit maximization.

THE GROWTH OF SCIENTIFIC MANAGEMENT

The emergence of a diffuse and complex private enterprise economic system directed by hired managers provided the stimulus for systematic study of management problems. The precursor of analytical approaches to management decision making was Frederick W. Taylor, one of the first industrial engineers and the founder of the "scientific management" school of thought.

Prior to Taylor's study, a number of workers were brought together to perform similar work at a uniform rate of pay by the day. Taylor observed this and termed it a systematic soldiering of workers.[3] One of the salient dysfunctions of this system was that the poorest worker tended to establish the amount of output for all the others. To further compound this situation, the existing method of establishing rates was based entirely on a foreman's concept of what constituted a day's output rather than accurate performance standards. If workers earned better than average pay, the day rates were cut. There was, therefore, a constant conflict between management and workers.

The workers attempted to gauge their output to earn as much as they could without getting the rates cut. Management, on the other hand, tried to induce the workers to increase their output to obtain lower costs.

Taylor's approach to this problem was a direct attack upon the pernicious method of establishing the output standards. These standards, he reasoned, should not be based upon a simple conceptualization of what constituted a day's output; rather they should be determined by careful study and observation of the tasks required to produce the firm's output. Once this was accomplished, the workers could be taught the most expeditious method of completing the required tasks. Workers completing a task in a period of time less than that allotted to it would receive a monetary reward called an incentive. It was assumed that the incentive would induce workers to increase their output. Taylor summarized the expected results as follows:[4]

Since (under the Taylor system) the rate-fixing is done from accurate knowledge instead of more or less by guesswork, the motive for holding back on work, for "soldiering" and endeavoring to deceive the employer as to time required to do the work, is entirely removed, and, with it, the greatest cause for hard feelings and war between the management and the men.

The essence of Taylor's "scientific management" was that the proper establishment of work standards, in combination with incentives for exceeding the standards, would encourage workers to produce more. He was concerned with the development and optimum operation of "men-machines." Speed, efficiency, selection, training, indoctrination, and incentives were the primary foci of his research. His major assumption was, of course, that the human organism could be transformed in such a way as to perform a job exactly as specified.[5]

THE HUMAN RELATIONS MOVEMENT

Taylor's major tenets became the guiding principles of management practices until the late 1920s. At this point, a series of experiments commonly referred to as the Hawthorne studies ushered in the human relations movement. These studies revealed that there was an array of "human factors" which contributed to overall worker satisfaction and, hence, to increased productivity and profitability of the firm.[6] The series of studies (of which we discuss only the important features) were conducted at the Hawthorne (Chicago) Works of the Western Electric Company between 1927 and 1932.

The Studies

From the beginning the experiments led to some surprising and perplexing findings. In one set of experiments, for example, illumination levels were systematically varied at work stations. The predicted results were that increased illumination would lead to increased productivity. The researchers found that no relationship existed between increased illumination and productivity. In a later experiment using workers placed in a control room, it was discovered that worker output did, in fact, increase as illumination increased, but it also continued to increase as illumination decreased. This perplexing finding forced the researchers to investigate the resultof manipulating other variables in the work environment.

They next decided to test the relationship between rest breaks and productivity. Workers placed in a control room were given rest periods of varying lengths and, as was predicted, production increased as the length of the rest period increased. The researchers also discovered, however, that production continued to increase in the experimental group when they were returned to the regular factory schedule. There was no evidence to support the hypothesis that increased rest periods would result in increased production.

At this point, the researchers began to conclude that there were no simple and direct relationships between the physical aspects of the work environment and increased productivity. It had been noted, however, that worker morale and motivation had been high because they felt important for having been chosen for the experiments. This suggested that a different kind of hypothesis was needed. The hypothesis was that worker productivity and morale are influenced by psychological and social factors. The finding that social and human factors in the work environment were often as important as the physical environment in influencing workers' productivity was to become the crucial discovery of the Hawthorne studies.

Discovery of Group Influence

In order to make a systematic and detailed investigation of the hypothesis, a new group consisting of nine wiremen, three soldermen, and two inspectors was chosen. These men were engaged in the assembly of terminal banks for telephone switchboards. They were taken out of their regular departments and placed in a special room where they could be observed by a trained observer who was installed in the room. After an initial period of suspicion of the observer, the workers relaxed and fell into their normal work routines. In this manner the now famous Bank Wiring Observation Room experiment was set up. It was in existence for seven months and contributed all of the important breakthroughs in the Hawthorne studies.

The following are the major findings and conclusions:

Finding 1. The level of effort and output is often set by group norms. While the Western Electric management had established an elaborate incentive system through which the individual could increase his earnings, the workers in the bank wiring room established their own standards of output. Two equipments a day were considered "a fair day's work for a fair day's pay." Although the group's standard of performance satisfied management's prediction of output, it was well below their physical capacity.

This finding was, of course, in direct contrast to the implicit assumption of the scientific management theorists that the relevant unit of analysis for the accomplishment of work is the individual. If this were true, then each worker in the bank wiring room would have pursued his economic interest by increasing not only his own output, but the output of every other worker in the group.

Finding 2. Group rewards and group sanctions limit the effectiveness of systems designed to relate extrinsic rewards to job productivity. The wage incentive system devised by management did not work because the work group had evolved its own norms regarding "a fair day's work." Whether the members of the group accepted or did not accept this norm, however, depended upon the strength of the rewards and punishment related to acceptance. The group rewarded a worker's conformity by providing him support, encouragement, and security. Deviates, on the other hand, were subjected to varying amounts of social pressures, such as sarcastic rebukes for being a "rate buster," or producing too little and being a "chiseler."

The bank wiring room workers clearly preferred the benefits derived from group membership to the monetary reward they would have received for increased output. The social benefits derived from group membership, such as acceptance and support, were more powerful motivators of work behavior than money.

Conclusion. The Hawthorne experiments dramatically illustrated the power of work groups to influence member actions toward various group standards and norms, i.e., groups invariably develop common values and behavioral expectations to which it is expected that their members will conform.[7]

What the experiments brought home to industrial managers was the realization that they could not treat workers only as individuals. Job productivity, in other words, was not only related to individual effort and reward, but to a diverse number of group social interactions. Therefore, compensation systems which ignored group influences could be rendered ineffective, particularly when management objectives did not coincide with those of the group. While the findings of the Hawthorne experiments were important to management, perhaps their lasting contribution was the impetus to form the so-called "human relations" movement. Since the experiments left as many questions unanswered as they answered, there was a need for broadening the knowledge deemed relevant to modern management.

Scientific Management v. Human Behavior

Whereas scientific management has concerned itself with efficiency and technically correct organization as the means for achieving worker productivity, the human relationists have stressed group relationships. The human relationists, moreover, have argued that overemphasis on the technology of the workplace has reduced productivity because social needs have been ignored. The scientific management school has countered that overemphasis on social needs has impaired productivity by forgetting profits.

While disagreement between the two schools of thought continues today, they have both made significant contributions to management thinking. The scientific management school continues to refine sophisticated incentive systems based upon industrial engineering standards. The human relations school, on the other hand, has expanded management knowledge on morale, social relationships, worker attitudes, and channels of communication.

THE BEHAVIORAL SCIENCE MOVEMENT

While the work of the human relationists continues today, their work has been augmented in more recent years by the behavioral scientists. They have perhaps become the more prominent exponents of the study of human factors in industrial organizations. Their increased use of theory most often distinguishes them from the human relationists, and for this reason we may consider them a separate school of thought. The behaviorists have not limited themselves to group behavior but have also contributed knowledge on the behavior of the individual in the organization. A brief description of individual behavior and its importance to management is provided by a behaviorist in the section which follows.[8]

Individual Behavior in the Organization

An understanding of individual behavior is an important contribution to management thought by the behaviorists, because it is necessary for controlling and predicting individual responses. In order to do so, however, a manager must operate with the proper set of assumptions concerning human behavior.

Theory X. Douglas McGregor added credence to these comments through his concept that managerial decisions or actions are governed by the assumptions managers make about human nature; he identified two primary categories of assumptions denoted as Theory X and Theory Y.[9] The Theory X assumptions include the views that the average human being has an inherent dislike of work and attempts to avoid it; that most persons must, therefore, be coerced to work; and that the average human being prefers to be directed and to avoid responsibility because he has little ambition and wants security above all else.

While the Theory X assumptions may provide an explanation of some human behavior in industry, there are many examples of behavior in industry which are not consistent with this view. The Theory X assumptions, in other words, might be correct if the individual's only needs were for a job and the monetary rewards associated with it.[10] Completely ignored, however, are the individual's higher level of needs, e.g., esteem of fellows, belongingness, satisfaction, and self-fulfillment. Thus, complete managerial reliance on Theory X assumptions would lead to some invalid predictions of human behavior.

Theory Y. In contrast to Theory X, the assumptions of Theory Y are that work itself may be a source of human satisfaction; that man may exercise self-direction and self-control in the service of objectives to which he is committed; that such commitment is a function of the rewards associated with the achievement of these objectives, the most significant of which may be ego satisfaction and self-actualization; that most human beings accept and seek responsibility under proper conditions; that imagination and ingenuity are distributed widely among workers; and that the intellectual potential the average human being is only partially utilized.

These assumptions promote a very different type of management, i.e., one which seeks to establish an environment within which the employee may realize his full potential. Individual participation is sought through techniques of group leadership. The manager is a coordinator of work. This participation is designed to make the individual's work meaningful and ego-satisfying. It integrates the need of the individual with those of the organization.[11]

THE FUTURE

The administration of a modern business enterprise has become an enormously complex undertaking. The major trend during the last 20 years has been the expansion of knowledge considered necessary to management. Since each of the schools of thought has contributed its own body of knowledge as a tool of management decision making, however, there is a current need to integrate the many sets of management ideologies. Perhaps this will be the next trend.

Another important trend in management thought is an increasing tendency to turn to quantitative techniques as a potential means for solving some of the problems that arise in complex enterprises. Quantitative management becomes increasingly more necessary in judging the relative merits of a variety of possible courses of action.

IMPORTANT NEW TERMS INTRODUCED

Day rate: A uniform rate of pay by the day.

Standardization: A uniform method for completing a required task.

Incentive: A monetary reward for completing a task in less time than that allotted to it.

Norm: A principle of correct action agreed upon by the members of a group.

SUGGESTED ADDITIONAL READINGS

Robert Dubin, *Human Relations in Administration*, Part II, 2nd ed. (Englewood Cliffs: Prentice-Hall, 1961).

William F. Whyte, *Men at Work* (Homewood: Richard D. Irwin, 1961).

NOTES

[1] See Rhinehart Bendix, *Work and Authority in Industry: Ideologies of Management in the Court of Industrialization* (New York: John Wiley, 1956).

[2] John Stuart Mill, *Principles of Political Economy,* (New York: D. Appleton; London, ed., 1878), pp. 420-421.

[3] See Frederick W. Taylor, *Principles of Scientific Management,* (New York: Harper, 1911).

[4] Ibid., p. 15.

[5] While Taylor's work concentrated on management problems at the shop level, another school of management thought, the "functional school," concentrated on the problems of upper management. The brevity of this chapter does not permit treatment, but the student may wish to read the work of the founding father of the school, Henri Fayol, *General and Industrial Management,* translation from the French (London: Isaac Pitman and Sons, 1949).

[6] A comprehensive account of this research is F. J. Roethlisberger and W. J. Dickson, *Management and the Worker* (Cambridge: Harvard University Press, 1939).

[7] For a detailed account of the bank wiring room study and the conclusions, see Committee on Work in Industry National Research Council, *Fatigue of Workers: Its Relation to Industrial Production* (New York: Reinhold Publishing Corp., 1941), pp. 77-86.

[8] The student interested in reading further in the area of individual behavior in the organization is referred to D. R. Hampton, C. E. Summer, and R. A. Weber, *Organizational Behavior and the Practice of Management* (Atlanta: Scott, Foresman, 1968), pp. 102-182.

[9] See Douglas McGregor, *The Human Side of Enterprise* (New York: McGraw-Hill, 1960), pp. 33-48.

[10] An interesting study on the type of individuals more highly motivated by money than social needs is provided in William F. Whyte et al., *Money and Motivation* (New York: Harper, 1955).

[11] A conceptual framework of an individual's needs is provided by A. H. Maslow, *Motivation and Personality* (New York: Harper, 1954).

Index

A

Adult Basic Education Program, 30
Adversary relationship, 122-24
Affirmative action (*see* Equal employment opportunity legislation)
Agency shop, 97
Allowances, family, 32-33
Amalgamated Association of Iron, Steel, and Tin Workers (*see* Unions)
American Arbitration Association, 115 (*see also* Grievances)
American Federation of Labor (*see* Unions)
American Federation of Labor-Congress of Industrial Organizations (*see* Unions)
American Plan, The, 55
American Railway Union (*see* Unions)
Anti-Injunction Act of 1932 (*see* Unions)
Apex v. Leader (1940), 86
Arbitration (*see* Grievances)
Armour and Company, 99-100
Assistance, public (*see* Public Assistance)

B

Behavioral science movement:
  individual behavior, 147-48
  Theory X and *Theory Y*, 147-48
  use of theories, 147
  (*see also* Management)
Benefits, fringe (*see* Fringe benefits)
Blind, Aid to the, 28 (*see also* Public Assistance)
Boston Journeymen Bootmakers Society (*see* Unions)
Boston police strike, 54, 117-18

C

Checkoff, dues (*see* Dues checkoff)
Children, Aid to Families with Dependent (*table*), 28 (*see also* Public Assistance)
Civil Rights Act of 1964, 38-39, 41
Clayton Antitrust Act, 82-83, 87

Unions *(cont.)*
boycotts, 81, 84, 86-87, 95
central bodies, 67-68
characteristics, 3, 73-74
  bargaining issues, 74
  jurisdiction, 51-52
  political activity, 74
  structure and government, 73-74
Committee for Industrial Organization, 56
company, 55
Congress of Industrial Organizations, 55
development, 77-89
  and conspiracy doctrine, 49, 78-79
  and wage ceilings, 78
dual, 56
Federal Society of Journeymen
    Cordwainers, 78-79
Industrial Workers of the World, 53
injunctions against, 80, 82-83
international, 65-66
  president, 66
  secretary-treasurer, 66
  vice-presidents, 66
International Brotherhood of Electrical
    Workers, 109-10
International Brotherhood of Teamsters,
    Chauffers, Warehousemen, and
    Helpers of America, 108-9
International Longshoremen's Union, 58
Knights of Labor, 51
local, 63-65
  federal, 56
  president, 65
  secretary-treasurer, 65
  shop stewards, 65
membership, 68-70
  attitudes, 71-73
  distribution *(table)*, 69
  growth *(chart)*, 72
  percentage of nonagricultural labor force
    (table), 69
  white-collar and nonproduction, 73
as monopolies, 80-81
organizing goals, 70-71
public employee, 129-31
public opinion, 70
Retail Clerks International Association,
    73

union shop, 96-97
United Automobile, Aerospace, and Agri-
    cultural Implement Workers, 49, 100
United Mine Workers of America, 52, 56
United Paperworkers International Union,
    108
United Steelworkers of America, 52
United Automobile Workers *(see* Unions)
United Labor Policy Committee, 58
United Mine Workers *(see* Unions)
United Mine Workers v. Pennington, 136
United Paperworkers International Union
    (see Unions)
*United Steelworkers of America v. Gulf and
    Warrior Navigation Company,* 107
U.S. Department of Commerce *(see* Com-
    merce, U.S. Department of)
U.S. Department of Labor *(see* Labor, U.S.
    Department of)
U.S. v. Hutcheson, 86-87

V

VISTA, 30
Voluntary Assistance Program, 30

W

Wages *(see* Collective bargaining)
Wagner, Robert, 85
Wagner Act, 56, 57, 84-87, 89
Wagner-Pyser Act of 1932, 41-42
War Labor Board, 57
War on Poverty, 22, 29
Welfare *(see* Public Assistance)
Wilson, Woodrow, 54
Wolman, Leo, 52, 54
Workmen's Compensation, 23-24
World War I, 54
World War II, 57

Y

Yellow-dog contracts, 84